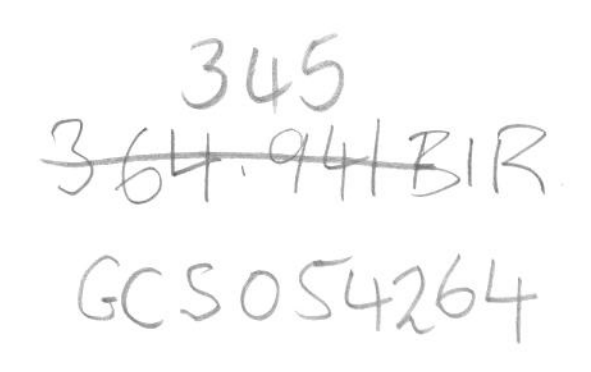

Crime in the UK

Editor: Tracy Biram

Volume 366

Independence Educational Publishers

First published by Independence Educational Publishers
The Studio, High Green
Great Shelford
Cambridge CB22 5EG
England

Copyright

Photocopy licence

ISBN-13: 978 1 86168 823 1

Printed in Great Britain

Zenith Print Group

Contents

Introduction

Crime in the UK is Volume 366 in the ***ISSUES*** series. The aim of the series is to offer current, diverse information about important issues in our world, from a UK perspective.

ABOUT CRIME IN THE UK

Have UK crime rates fallen or risen over recent years? There are many conflicting reports and viewpoints on this matter. This book explores the latest statistics showing which crimes are falling and which crimes are on the rise. It also focuses on knife crime, particularly in relation to young people and it takes a look at the justice system and current measures being taken to combat crime.

OUR SOURCES

Titles in the ***ISSUES*** series are designed to function as educational resource books, providing a balanced overview of a specific subject.

The information in our books is comprised of facts, articles and opinions from many different sources, including:

- Newspaper reports and opinion pieces
- Website factsheets
- Magazine and journal articles
- Statistics and surveys
- Government reports
- Literature from special interest groups.

A NOTE ON CRITICAL EVALUATION

Because the information reprinted here is from a number of different sources, readers should bear in mind the origin of the text and whether the source is likely to have a particular bias when presenting information (or when conducting their research). It is hoped that, as you read about the many aspects of the issues explored in this book, you will critically evaluate the information presented.

It is important that you decide whether you are being presented with facts or opinions. Does the writer give a biased or unbiased report? If an opinion is being expressed, do you agree with the writer? Is there potential bias to the 'facts' or statistics behind an article?

ASSIGNMENTS

In the back of this book, you will find a selection of assignments designed to help you engage with the articles you have been reading and to explore your own opinions. Some tasks will take longer than others and there is a mixture of design, writing and research-based activities that you can complete alone or in a group.

FURTHER RESEARCH

At the end of each article we have listed its source and a website that you can visit if you would like to conduct your own research. Please remember to critically evaluate any sources that you consult and consider whether the information you are viewing is accurate and unbiased.

Useful Websites

www.birminghammail.co.uk
www.crimestoppers.co.uk
www.fearless.org
www.fullfact.org
www.gov.uk
www.howardleague.org
www.inews.co.uk
www.justyouth.org.uk
www.noknivesbetterlives.co.uk
www.ons.gov.uk
www.researchbriefings.parliament.uk
www.shoutoutuk.org
www.theconversation.com
www.theguardian.com
www.telegraph.co.uk
www.youthlinkscotland.org

Crime in England and Wales: year ending June 2019

Latest bulletin from the Crime Survey for England and Wales (CSEW) and the Office for National Statistics (ONS).

Main points

Overall levels of crime showed falls in recent decades, but have remained broadly stable in recent years. While in the last year there has been no change in overall levels of crime, this hides variation seen in individual crime types. The latest figures show a mixed picture, with continued rises in some types of theft, 'bank and credit account fraud' and falls in 'computer viruses'. There were also increases in some of the less frequently occurring but higher-harm types of violence, including offences involving knives or sharp instruments.

Headline figures

The Crime Survey for England and Wales (CSEW) indicated a continuing rise in fraud with the latest estimates showing a 15% increase, driven by a 17% rise in 'bank and credit account fraud'.

All other main crime types measured by CSEW showed no change, including lower-harm violent offences (for example, violence without injury and assault with minor injury). However, police-recorded crime gives more insight into the lower-volume but higher-harm violence that the survey either does not cover or does not capture well. These data show:

- a 5% decrease in the number of homicides following a period of increases over the last four years
- a 4% increase in the number of police-recorded offences involving firearms
- a 7% increase[1] in the number of police-recorded offences involving knives or sharp instruments.

Many of these lower-volume, higher-harm types of violence tend to be concentrated in metropolitan areas such as London, the West Midlands, West Yorkshire and Greater Manchester.

While the total number of offences involving knives or sharp instruments increased in England and Wales, the number of homicides where a knife or sharp instrument was involved decreased by 14%. This decrease was mainly driven by falls in London. There is a mixed picture in the total number of offences involving knifes or sharp instruments across different police force areas, with the Metropolitan Police recording little change in the last year.

Although the latest estimate of theft offences measured by CSEW showed no change in the last year, there was an 11% increase when compared with the year ending March 2017. While CSEW provides the better indication of overall trends in theft offences, police-recorded crime data can help identify short-term changes in individual offences that are thought to be well-reported and accurately recorded by the police. In the latest year these data show:

- a 3% increase in vehicle offences, which includes a 7% rise in the subcategory of 'theft or unauthorised taking of a motor vehicle'
- an 11% increase in robbery
- a 4% decrease in burglary.

Note for: Main points

1. Excludes Greater Manchester Police (GMP) because of a technical issue that resulted in previous undercounting of crimes involving a knife or sharp instrument. GMP have now changed their methodology and data from December 2017 onwards have been revised. As a result of these changes data for GMP are not comparable over this time.

What do the latest figures show?

	Figures for year ending June 2019, compared with previous survey year	Things to note
Computer misuse	No change in computer misuse offences as estimated by CSEW, although there was a 27% decrease in 'computer viruses' to 442,000 offences.	The Crime Survey for England and Wales (CSEW) is the best source for measuring the volume of computer misuse offences as it captures offences that go unreported. However, as computer misuse is a recent addition to the CSEW and only limited time series data are available, caution must be taken in interpreting early trends. Computer misuse offences include computer viruses as well as 'unauthorised access to personal information (including hacking)'.
Criminal damage and arson	No change in overall criminal damage and arson estimated by the CSEW (1,082,000 offences).	Police-recorded criminal damage and arson offences have seen little change in the last year (3% decrease to 568,131 offences).
Domestic abuse	According to the CSEW, there was no change in the proportion of adult victims experiencing domestic abuse in the year ending March 2019 (6.3%) compared with the previous year (6.1%). Of all crimes recorded by the police, 14% were flagged as domestic abuse-related.	Given the different factors affecting the reporting and recording of these offences, the police figures do not provide a reliable measure of current trends. The CSEW is the better source for domestic abuse victimisation.
Fraud	The CSEW estimated a 15% increase in fraud offences (to 3,863,000 offences). This increase is driven mainly by increases in bank and credit account fraud (17%, to 2,666,000 offences) and 'other fraud' (183%, to 188,000 offences).	The CSEW provides the best indication of the volume of fraud offences experienced by individuals as it captures the more frequent lower-harm cases that are likely to go unreported to the authorities. However, as fraud is a recent addition to the CSEW and only limited time series data are available, caution must be taken in interpreting early trends.
Homicide	There was a 5% decrease in police recorded homicide offences (from 719 to 681 offences). There was a 14% decrease in police-recorded homicides involving a knife or sharp instrument (287 to 248 offences).	Trends in homicide can be affected by events with multiple homicide victims, such as the recorded victims of Harold Shipman. No such events occurred in the year ending June 2018 or June 2019.
Public order offences	Police-recorded public order offences increased by 9% (to 445,945 offences).	A large part of this increase is likely to reflect improvements to recording practices. For example, incidents that may have previously been recorded as an anti-social behaviour incident may now be recorded as a public order offence. It is also possible that genuine increases in public disorder may also have contributed to the rise.

Robbery	Police-recorded robbery offences saw an 11% increase (to 88,177 offences).	This increase is likely to reflect some real change in these crimes. Recording improvements are likely to have contributed, but the impact is thought to be less pronounced than for some other crime types. The CSEW does not provide a robust measure of short-term trends in robbery as it is a relatively low-volume crime. The offence of robbery involves theft (or attempted theft) with the use or threat of force. However, it forms a standalone category, separate from theft.
Sexual offences	According to the CSEW, there was no change in the proportion of adults who experienced sexual assaults in the year ending March 2019 (2.9%) compared with the previous year (2.7%). Over the longer term, there was a rise in sexual assault estimated by the survey over the past five years, with the latest estimate returning to levels similar to those around a decade ago.	Given the different factors affecting the reporting and recording of these offences, the police figures do not provide a reliable measure of current trends. The CSEW is the better source of victimisation data on sexual offences.
Theft offences	No change in overall theft offences estimated by the CSEW (3,690,000 offences) in the latest year, but an 11% rise compared with the year ending March 2017. Vehicle offences recorded by the police increased by 3% to 469,915. This was mainly the result of increases in 'theft or unauthorised taking of a motor vehicle' (7%, to 115,777) and 'theft from a vehicle' (2%, to 284,225). Burglary offences recorded by the police saw a 4% decrease to 417,416, driven mainly by decreases in 'residential burglary' (5%, to 291,816). There was a 10% increase in 'theft from a person' offences recorded by the police, to 109,096.	The CSEW provides the better indication of overall trends in theft offences. It better captures more minor thefts, such as from outside a dwelling, which are less likely to be reported to the police. However, police-recorded crime data can help identify short-term changes in individual offences. Vehicle offences and burglary offences are thought to be generally well-reported by victims and well-recorded by the police Additionally, as with 'robbery', 'theft from the person' is also a low-volume crime. Therefore, CSEW estimates are prone to greater fluctuations than estimates for more frequently occurring offences. Although this offence is prone to changes in recording practices, the police-recorded data can often be a better measure of short-term trends than CSEW.
Violence and weapons offences	No change in overall violent offences estimated by the CSEW (1,327,000 offences). Police-recorded offences involving a knife or sharp instrument increased by 7% (to 44,076 offences). This figure excludes Greater Manchester Police (GMP). The rate of increase has fallen from 14% in the year ending June 2018. Police-recorded offences involving firearms saw a 4% increase (to 6,734 offences), driven by rises in offences involving weapons such as stun guns, CS gas and pepper spray, partly reflecting improvements in identifying these cases.	The CSEW provides the better indication of overall trends in violent crime, giving a good measure of the more common but less harmful offences. Police-recorded crime provides a better measure of the more harmful but less common offences. Such offences are not well-measured by the survey because of their relatively low volume GMP have changed their methodology after identifying an undercount of crimes involving a knife or sharp instrument. Data for GMP are not comparable over this time period. Including GMP, there were 47,513 knife or sharp instrument offences. It is possible that recording improvements in other forces have also contributed to the increase.

www.ons.gov.uk

Youth crime on the rise in the UK

Will a recent change in the law really make a difference?

By Anoop Bhuller

Police statistics have shown that knife and gun-related crimes increased by an overwhelming 14 per cent just last year. Youth crime is increasing in the UK which begs the question whether the law is effective for the younger generations in today's society. The Youth Justice Statistics, published in January 2018, show that there was a staggering 14,500 new entrants into the Youth Justice System. This alone shows the extent to which youth crimes have increased, emphasising the importance for changes to be made to the law.

There were 40,000 proven offences involving possession of a knife or offensive weapon. Knife crime is often associated with gangs in the UK. Since the release of this report the knife laws in the UK have been changed. Now, anyone that buys a knife online will be banned from having it sent to a residential address. We can only wait to see if this law will be effective in reducing youth crime.

At the time when Amber Rudd was still the home secretary, she created a ban on acid sales to under 18s. This law may help youth gangs from using acid in their crimes. Although these measures had been taken as a strategy to reducing crime, there are still daily cases of youth crimes being reported. In fact, there has been a known increase in the amount of moped muggings taking place in the UK. This type of crime poses a great threat, as approaching a pedestrian on a motorbike could potentially cause physical harm to the victim. As the criminals are on motorbikes it makes it harder for them to be stopped or identified, given that their faces are always covered with helmets or masks.

Therefore, new laws should be put in place in order to try and tackle this particular crime. There are still youth gangs present throughout Britain. Education on youth crime should be implemented in schools so that young people are aware of the personal risk and consequences involved when being in a youth gang. Early education and awareness of crimes could prevent young people becoming involved in illegal activity. A more proactive approach should be implemented in schools when it comes to educating the youth about the importance of avoiding crime.

Young people are aware that some crimes can be cleared once they turn 18, this may be one explanation for the increase in gangs: kids think that they will not have to become accountable for their actions and will be given a clean slate once they turn 18. However, the law actually states that the likelihood of a youth's record being erased depends on the seriousness of the offence, the sentence they received and any other possible offenses they may have made. This is something that should be emphasised to young people.

In order to reduce youth crime, the causes of young people committing crimes need to be fully understood. These causes could include peer pressure, family troubles, bullying, financial hardship, as well as drug and alcohol abuse. In addition to this, young people feel astounding pressure nowadays to feel part of a group. Tackling these issues would lower youth crime and encourage young people to create a stable life for themselves. Arguably, if young people felt more supported, it would deter them from making bad decisions. It is necessary for authority figures to show young people that making the right moral decision will lead to a more rewarding life. If youths understand this, they will be less keen to join gangs or participate in crimes.

30 October 2018

Police officer numbers in England and Wales

The number of police officers in England and Wales has fallen by over 20,000 between March 2010 and March 2018.

There were over 122,000 police officers in March this year. Counting those from the British Transport Police and those on secondment it was 126,000.

These figures refer to the number of full time equivalent officers (or how many there would be if you added up all their hours to make full -time roles).

The number of police officers in England and Wales is the lowest recorded level since the early 1980s. To make a consistent comparison over time, we have to use figures from March each year. Policing is local too, though. If you live in Merseyside, you won't be directly affected by what's happening to police numbers in Gwent.

The staffing picture varies across the 43 police forces of England and Wales. 51% of forces have gained officers in the year to March 2018, with Humberside Police seeing the biggest rise in numbers (a 9% increase). 47% have lost officers, with West Mercia seeing the biggest drop (a 4% decrease). One force saw no change.

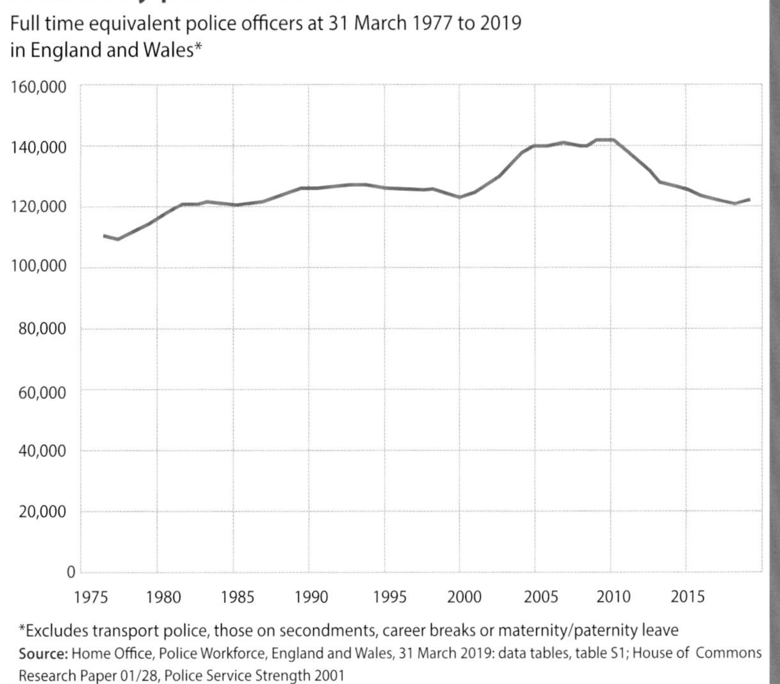

How many police officers?

Full time equivalent police officers at 31 March 1977 to 2019 in England and Wales*

*Excludes transport police, those on secondments, career breaks or maternity/paternity leave

Source: Home Office, Police Workforce, England and Wales, 31 March 2019: data tables, table S1; House of Commons Research Paper 01/28, Police Service Strength 2001

How many frontline officers?

Full time equivalent police officers in frontline roles at 31 March 2010 to 2019 in England and Wales*

140,000
120,000
100,000
80,000
60,000
40,000
20,000
0
2010 2011 2012 2013 2014 2015 2016 2017 2018 2019

*Figures for 2010 – 2014 are estimates

Source: Home Office, Police Workforce, England and Wales, 31 March 2019: data tables, table F5

You might also care about the number of frontline officers. There's no hard and fast definition of who fits that description. The official definition has changed several times.

At the moment, officers are categorised as one of frontline (like response teams, neighbourhood policing and front desk roles), frontline support (such as intelligence), business support (such as training) or not coded (such as national policing).

Using that breakdown, there are 16% fewer 'frontline' officers since 2010.

Again, that varies. Police forces structure and record their roles differently so it's tricky to directly compare them, but in March 2018 the City of London categorised 71% of police officers as frontline, while in Cheshire it was 94%.

11 September 2018

Homicides in England reach highest level in a decade

Figures show knife crime is up 6% and proportion of offenders being charged has fallen.

By Vikram Dodd, Police and Crime Correspondent

Homicides are at a record high for the past decade, knife crime is rising and the proportion of offenders being charged has reached a record low, two sets of official figures show. The Office for National Statistics said that in the year to December 2018, 732 lives were lost to homicide, compared with 690 the previous year. The figure is the highest number recorded since 2008. Homicide includes murder, manslaughter, corporate manslaughter and infanticide.

The total covers both England and Wales, although in Wales homicides fell from 35 in 2017 to 27 in 2018.

Offences involving knives rose 6%, with police recording 40,829, the highest number the ONS has on record since 2011.

One-third of knife offences were in London and use of bladed weapons was concentrated in urban areas, the ONS said, but there were some signs the increase was slowing.

The ONS said all 43 forces had seen increases in violent offences, including an 11% rise in reported rapes, 46% in stalking, 11% for robbery, 12% in fraud and 8% for theft.
The ONS said the picture was mixed, with no significant change in overall crime and some apparent falls in certain offences.

Firearms offences fell 2% to 6,525 recorded incidents, burglary declined by 3% to 424,846 offences, and computer misuse dropped 28% to 976,000 offences, with fewer devices being infected by viruses, the ONS said. Overall, crime year on year rose 2%, which the ONS said was not statistically significant.
In its commentary, the ONS said people in England and Wales were now less likely to experience any type of crime than in the mid-1990s. 'The likelihood of being a victim of crime has fallen considerably over the long term,' it said.

'Around 40 in 100 adults were estimated to have been a victim of crime in 1995. This was before the survey included fraud and computer misuse in its coverage. Based on crimes comparable with those measured in the 1995 survey, 15 in 100 adults were victims of crime in the year ending December 2018,' the ONS added.

Alexa Bradley from the ONS centre for crime and justice said: 'When we look at the overall level of crime, there has been no significant change over the last year.

'However, it is important to look at each crime type separately because the picture is very mixed. Even within crime types we have seen differences. Robbery and vehicle offences have increased, whereas burglary has decreased. Lower-volume, high-harm violence involving knives has risen, whereas offences involving firearms have decreased.'

Crime has become a politically charged issue, with Labour and many in the police blaming government cuts for crime increasing as officer numbers have fallen. The complex figures and the morass of crime data allow different conclusions to be drawn, but what does emerge are rises in the most serious offences, some of which are at record levels. The policing minister, Nick Hurd, said: 'Today's statistics show that your chance of being a victim of crime remains low.

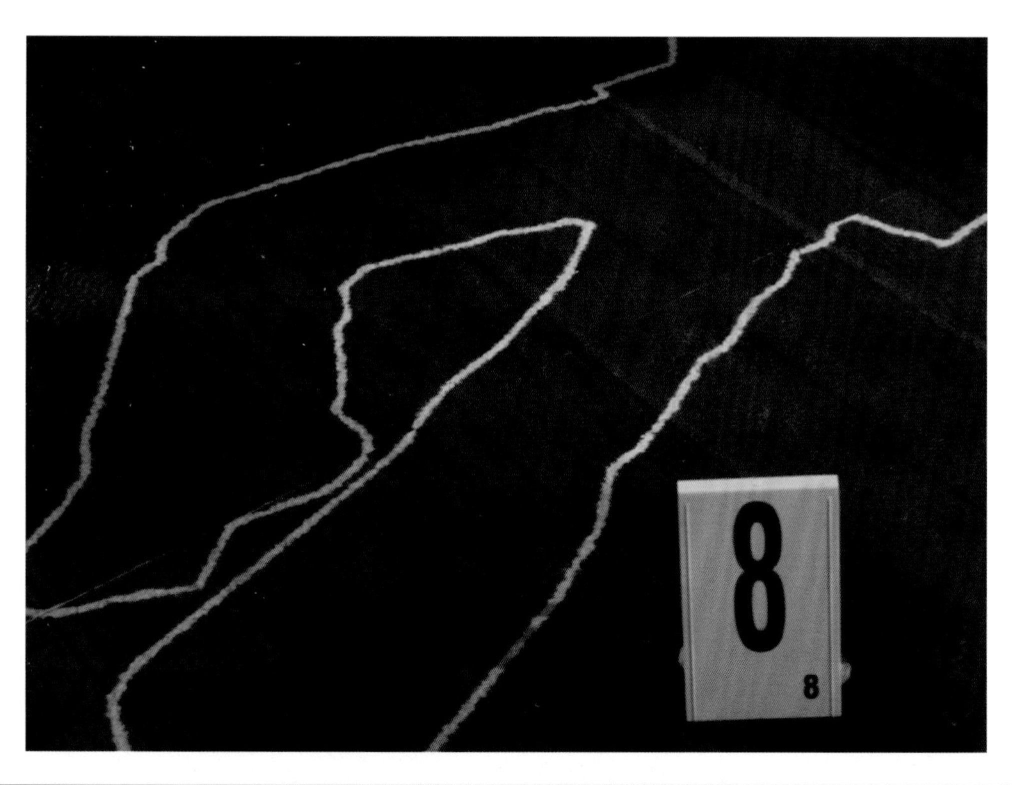

'Yet too many people are still falling victim to serious violence, which is why we will continue our urgent and unprecedented action to reverse this terrible trend.

'We have given police forces additional powers and have this year put more than £1 billion extra into policing, including

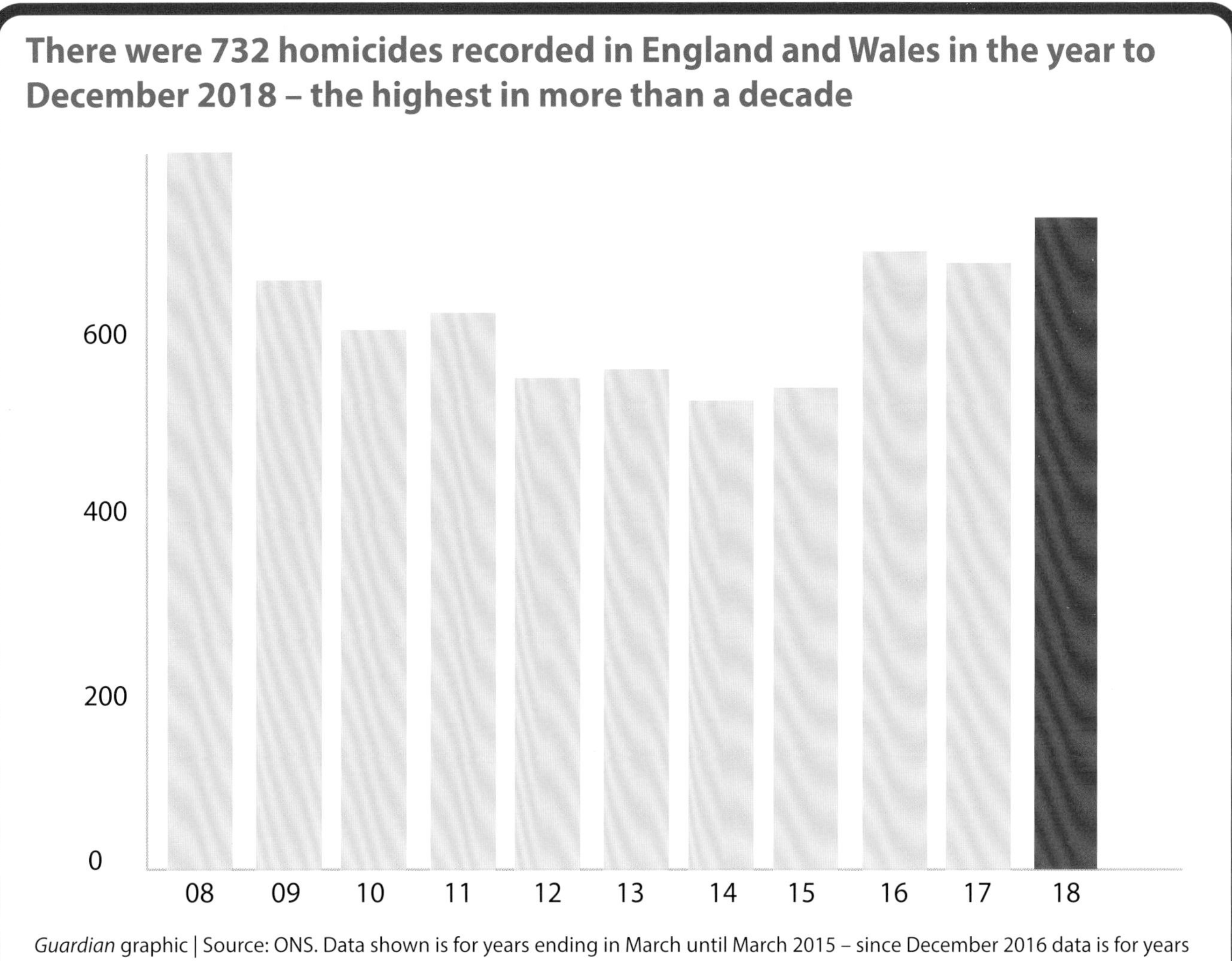

Guardian graphic | Source: ONS. Data shown is for years ending in March until March 2015 – since December 2016 data is for years ending in December

council tax, and £100 million specifically for those areas worst affected by violent crime.'

Separate Home Office figures show the proportion of crimes leading to charges or summons falling to 8.2% of the total volume of crimes. It is the joint lowest figure since recording began of those figures in 2002–3.

In more than 1 million incidents, victims did not support action – 22% of offences in the year to December 2018.

For rape, just 1.7% of reported offences led to someone being charged or summonsed, and the figure compared to attacks is likely to be worse because academics and police believe only a fraction of offences are reported. In 40% of cases, rape victims did not support further action.

Ché Donald of the Police Federation of England and Wales, which was accused of shroud-waving by the Government when it warned that cuts would lead to rising violence, said: "Despite the best efforts of our members, we have seen crime continue to increase, and the resultant demands placed on policing are unprecedented but unfortunately predictable.

'Crime across the board is going up. The only things that are not going up are police numbers, police pay and meaningful funding. The Government should be investing in our police service so we can get on with tackling this highly concerning situation. These figures must shame them into action.'

The Labour MP Yvette Cooper, who chairs the home affairs select committee, said: 'Knife crime is now at record levels and this is a very disturbing increase in violent crime at the same time as the number of arrests is continuing to fall.

'The police are completely overstretched and crime prevention work is far too limited.

'The Home Office and government response on knife crime and other rising crimes is still far too weak and just doesn't match the scale of the problem.'

25 April 2019

www.theguardian.com

Violent crime is not at record levels

In brief.

By Joseph O'Leary

Claim

Violent crime is at record levels.

'Never since records began have violent crime and knife crime been as high as they are today. This crisis is a consequence of nine years of government cuts to the police and youth services.'

– Louise Haigh MP on Twitter (@LouHaigh) 25 January 2019

It's not correct that violent crime is at a record high. Several reliable sources indicate that violent crime is far lower now than it was in the 1990s in England and Wales.

Louise Haigh's claims are based on the number of violent crimes recorded by the police. It's true that police figures show the highest ever recorded levels of violent crime and knife crime specifically, but it's almost impossible to derive any trustworthy trend from this data, as police recording practices have changed significantly over time.

This isn't to say violent crime isn't rising – the evidence indicates some types of violent crime have begun to increase in recent years. But saying violence is at record levels is flatly contradicted by more reliable data.

Looking at knife crime specifically, police and hospital figures show knife crime to be at or near its highest recorded levels. Knife crime is almost certainly rising at the moment, but no source is strong enough for us to be certain that it's at record levels.

Violent crime is difficult to measure accurately

Violent crime covers a broad range of crimes – from minor assaults (such as pushing and shoving) to murder.

Nobody knows exactly how many violent crimes are happening. Crimes are, by their nature, difficult to spot and count properly. That's why we have several sources of information to help us. When it comes to measuring violent crime, three sources are most relevant:

- What the police record as a result of their activity
- A survey of households (the Crime Survey for England and Wales) to find out people's experiences as victims of crime, which can detect crimes the police aren't noticing as well as what they are
- Hospital admissions for victims of assault – these indirectly indicate the amount of violence that's serious enough to leave someone attending hospital.

All three sources have their strengths and weaknesses. The police data is generally bad at telling us anything about trends over time. Not only do they not record all crime that actually happens (some crimes often go under-reported to the police), they've been subject to a lot of changes over the years in how the police count the data. The one thing it is more useful for is for crimes that happen very rarely and cause a high level of harm, like knife crimes or murder. But even in the case of knife crime, it's still very unreliable.

The Crime Survey is much better at telling us about trends, because it's always had a consistent methodology and can pick up crimes that go unreported to the police. But because it's a survey of households, it's less useful for picking up changes in crimes which don't happen very often, and doesn't tell us anything about crimes against businesses.

Hospital admissions are tangible examples of the impact of serious violent crimes, and are valuable to look at alongside police figures to compare the two. But it's only an indirect indicator – we don't know how many of the admissions are actually due to crimes, not least because recording accuracy can still vary, and they don't pick up lower-harm violence that doesn't leave people in hospital.

Violent crime in England and Wales is much lower today than in the 1990s

According to the Crime Survey for England and Wales, violent crime peaked in 1995 and has fallen by over two-thirds since then. In recent years, those falls have largely flattened out.

Nearly five in every 100 adults aged 16 and over were estimated to have been victims of violent crime in 1995. In 2016/17, fewer than two in 100 adults were.

Data from other sources backs up the Crime Survey

Figures from hospitals in England also show a falling trend since 2006/07. Back then, just under 46,000 admissions were recorded where the reason was believed to have been an assault (excluding sexual assault). By 2017/18, just over 28,000 such admissions were recorded. These figures only cover England, whereas the Crime Survey data also includes Wales. There's also been separate research from Cardiff University into attendances at accident and emergency units in England and Wales as a whole. This research also took the growing population into account and found a falling trend in attendances due to violence between 2002 and 2017.

While these figures aren't direct measures of crime trends, they do support the idea that violent crime today is less common than it used to be.

Both sources of figures are better indicators than police records. The Office for National Statistics (ONS) says that:

'For the population groups and offences it covers, the Crime Survey for England and Wales (CSEW) is the best source for

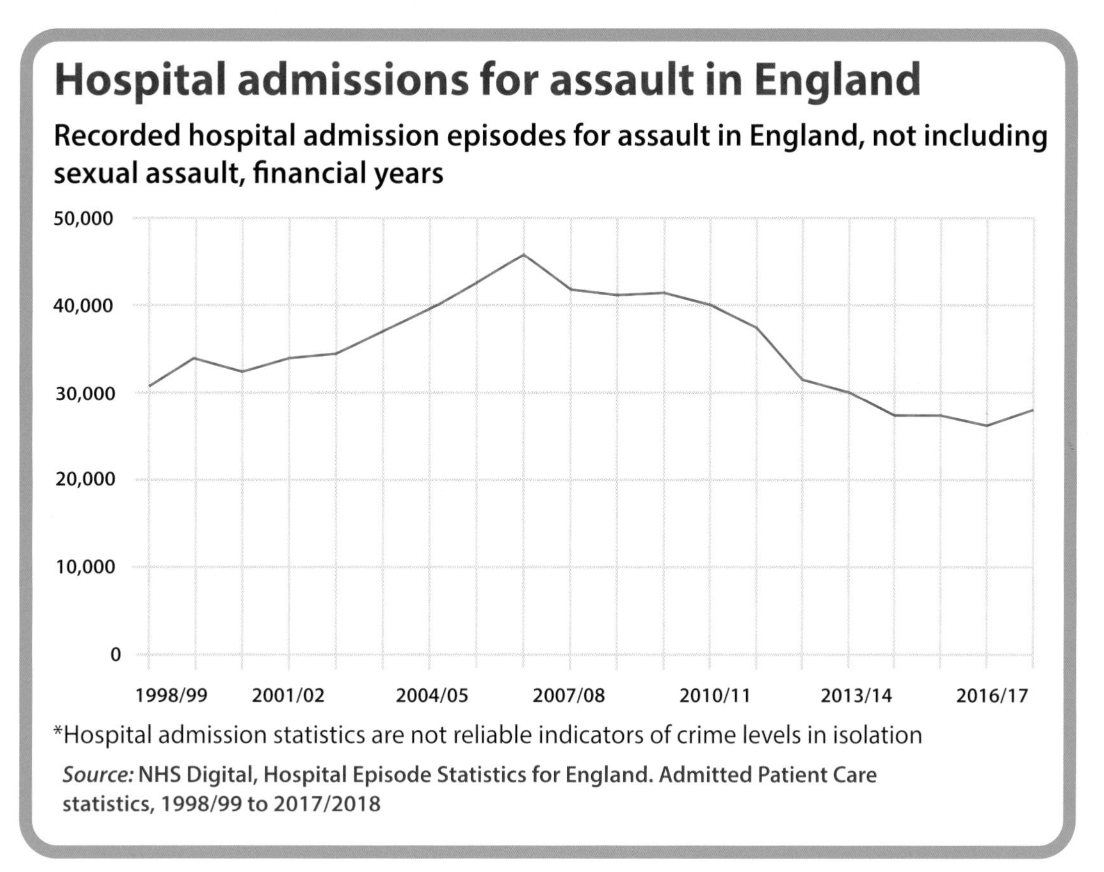

assessing long-term trends in violent crime as the survey's methodology has remained consistent over time.'

The police have never recorded more violent crimes

This statement sounds like it completely contradicts the previous one. But even though the police are recording more violent crimes than they ever have before, the weight of evidence suggests that it's not because violent crime is getting more common – it's just that the police have got better at recording it.

In fact, violent crime is believed to be one of the types of crime most affected by changes in police recording practices, particularly lower harm offences. Inspection reports into police forces also suggest some offences, like sexual offences, are still being under-recorded by forces.

In the year ending September 2018, the police recorded over 1.5 million violent crimes (called 'violence against the person'). Those figures don't include sexual offences – which are recorded separately – but sexual offences are also at their highest recorded levels.

The same is true if you take into account the rising population. In the mid-2000s, police records suggested the violent crime rate was about 16 incidents for every 1,000 people, compared to 26 per 1,000 in the year to September 2018.

Some kinds of violent crime are rising

Even though the police figures are generally unreliable, it's still likely that some kinds of violent crime are rising at the moment.

Louise Haigh also specifies knife crime: claiming that since records began knife crime has never been as high as it is today. This claim is on more solid ground. Police recorded knife crimes in England and Wales are at their highest level of around 40,000 a year – although comparable records only go back to 2010.

Again, however, the police force figures are known to have been affected by improvements to recording practices in recent years, so we don't have a certain picture of whether these are truly record levels.

Hospital admissions data also shows that admissions for assault by a sharp object are rising and at near-record levels.

The Crime Survey isn't as helpful here. Knife crime is a relatively rare offence, and offences like that are difficult to pick up reliably in a survey.

So we don't have enough evidence to say definitively whether knife crime is at record levels – but the claim is certainly backed up by stronger evidence than Ms Haigh's claims on violence in general

1 February 2019

Conclusion

Incorrect. Several reliable sources indicate that overall violent crime in England and Wales is far lower now than it was in the 1990s. Police figures show violent crimes at their highest recorded level, but these are unreliable.

www.fullfact.org

County lines: the dark realities of life for teenage drug runners

An article from **The Conversation.**

By Grace Robinson, PhD Candidate and Graduate Teaching Assistant, Edge Hill University

'County lines' is a term used by the police to describe a growing practice among criminal gangs: when demand for drugs fails to meet the supply in major cities, gangs travel to remote rural areas, market towns or coastal locations in search of new customers.

The process – referred to as 'going cunch' (country) or 'going OT' (out there) by those involved – has initiated ugly forms of exploitation. Children as young as 12 are hired as "runners" to transport and sell illicit drugs, while the homes of vulnerable adults are occupied without permission to create a base to sell from – a practice also known as 'cuckooing'.

Tackling county lines is now a national priority: the government has launched a new £3.6 million National County Lines Coordination Centre, made up of experts from the National Crime Agency. The centre aims to measure the threat of county lines, focus resources on the most serious offenders and work closely with partners in health, welfare and education to reduce the harms associated with the practice.

For our latest research, published in the *International Journal of Offender Therapy and Comparative Criminology*, we spoke with members of organised crime groups, police, staff on youth offending teams and young people aged between 14 and 17 involved in drugs gangs in Glasgow, Scotland and Merseyside, England, to find out what leads them to get involved in this practice, and how it affects their lives.

Working the lines

Before gangs started using the county lines model, class A drugs such as heroin and crack cocaine were typically supplied in remote areas by user-dealers who would sell to locals from their own supply. Competition in these areas was low, and violence was kept to a minimum

But in recent years, gangs have been using experience gained in the big cities to enter into smaller, satellite areas with high demand, good profit margins and low police presence. They are leveraging violent reputations earned in the big cities to intimidate and dominate existing players in the illegal drugs market. Police in picturesque county towns such as Shrewsbury (a town of about 70,000 people close to the Welsh border in Western England) are now dealing with turf wars and homicides.

During our research, we found that one of the root causes of this problem is how normal it is among teenagers to use cannabis – and the monetary cost of this. Young people in our study began smoking weed recreationally with their friends as young as 13. Perhaps more significant than the psychological and physical effects of cannabis use, which are heightened around the time of puberty, was the fact that weed cost money that these adolescents did not have.

The majority of county lines workers we interviewed in Merseyside owed money to a drug dealer. They accrued debt by having their drugs 'on tick' – a slang term for a 'buy now, pay later' scheme. When they failed to pay, the indebted were forced into working for their dealers. Working the lines meant being deployed anywhere at any time, answering the phone without delay when their masters (or clients) called, and leaving their post only to meet paying customers.

Debt bondage wasn't the only way people ended up working the lines. Some of our interviewees in Glasgow entered the trade by their own volition. They were willing to travel and simply asked known drug dealers for a job. Owing to boredom, poverty and a sense of hopelessness about their legitimate job prospects, these young people felt they had no choice but to sell drugs.

The experiences of young people who had made a choice (albeit a constrained one) to 'go country' didn't fully concur with the horror stories about the practice portrayed by the media. During their interviews, some young people recalled their experiences as 'funny', especially when they spoke of the exploitative relationships they had formed with vulnerable drug users.

Young interviewees in both cities recounted how drug users would be 'terrored' or intimidated to pass the time between waiting for the phone to ring and completing drug sales. Young people would entertain themselves by getting users to perform sex acts, eat from ashtrays and 'shit off the floor"' or undergo 'challenges' in exchange for 'free' drugs.

Removing root causes

Our findings expose a paradox at the heart of county lines – the exploited and the exploiters are often one and the same. Drug dealers, drug runners and drug users form a hierarchical structure, with the most vulnerable – the users – at the bottom. Drug runners look down on drug addicts to make themselves feel better about their own station.

County lines expose that drug prohibition is not working: current laws neither effectively prevent young people from selling drugs, nor protect the most vulnerable in society from consuming them. Positive initiatives such as the National County Lines Coordination Centre are necessary for sharing intelligence between police and social service providers, but constrained by the folly of existing drug policy.

Our research highlights that a criminal justice approach based on tough enforcement and recovering the proceeds of crime is not enough to dissuade dealers from dealing. Unless we tackle demand for illicit drugs, and the root causes of gang culture – namely social and economic marginalisation – county lines will continue to be drawn.

21 October 2018

Gangs (county lines)

A gang could simply be a group of friends that all like doing the same things. The word takes on a new meaning when a group of friends gets involved in criminal activity.

Although it is not illegal to be a member of a gang, much of the activity that criminal street gangs get caught up in is. If caught committing an offence you could end up with a longer sentence just for being part of a gang.

There are many different and complex reasons as to why people join gangs. It could be for status, to feel a sense of belonging, to make money, to earn respect or for protection from other gangs.

Status is a key factor that influences members of criminal street gangs. Having access to weapons provides a gang with an immediate status – as other rival gangs will be fearful. This is why many gangs pose with photos of guns and knives on their social networking sites – to 'show off' how easily they can access weapons.

It is illegal to carry a weapon and if caught they will face time in prison.

Many street gangs are involved with the supply and dealing of drugs. This can be a way that gangs make money. Dealing in drugs, like running a business, has many different roles and levels of people controlling the entire operation. One emerging operation negatively impacting the lives of thousands of young people is known as 'county lines'.

County lines

County lines (also known as 'going country') is a tactic used by individuals, or more commonly by groups/criminal gangs to establish a drug dealing operation in an area outside of their usual localities. This typically involves gangs moving their operations from large urban cities out into more remote rural areas – particularly coastal towns, market towns, or commuter towns close to large cities.

DID YOU KNOW?

Reasons for establishing outside of local areas

There are various reasons why drug dealers choose to move their operations outside of their usual areas, some of which are outlined below:

- For anonymity – county lines operations have been found to be set up across multiple police force boundaries, sometimes hundreds of miles away from the dealers' original locations, therefore making it harder to be detected by law enforcement. Furthermore, being that far away also makes it harder to be detected by their competitors and other rival gangs.
- A receptive customer base – customers in rural areas have limited access to drug supplies (in comparison to those in urban areas). Therefore there is more of a demand for the drugs in these areas than in the highly competitive urban areas where the dealers have come from.

- Less intimidating competition – it has been suggested that the prolific use of firearms by criminal gangs in urban areas means that supplying drugs outside of these areas reduces the chances of being a target. Therefore there is a perception that the competition in rural areas are less intimidating and easier to overcome.

Cuckooing

This refers to the process through which county lines operators take over a local property to use as a base for their criminal activity. The operators usually target and exploit vulnerable people such as those dependent on drugs, with mental health issues, or the elderly. Through the use of violence, intimidation, or coercion (i.e. by offering money or drugs in exchange of use of their property), the operators then take over the property, sometimes rendering the victim homeless in the process.

Vulnerable females have also been found to be exploited for the use of their property. Sometimes they are coerced into abusive relationships, offered low-priced drugs in order to gain control over them, and in other cases being prostituted and sexually assaulted, all the while taking over their homes in the process.

Exploitation of children as 'runners'

A commonly recurring theme in county lines is the exploitation of children and young people. County lines operators often groom and use young people as 'runners', making them carry drugs or money to and from the areas where the operation has been established. This is often via train but also by car and coaches.

Children are also often made to stay over at the location (known as 'the trap' or 'trap house') and made to distribute the drugs in the area.

Some criminal gangs, usually as part of gang initiation, are involved in sex crimes and there has been a significant increase in cases of gang rape in the UK over the past five years. The role and relationship of girls in criminal street gangs is very complex. Girls affiliated with gangs are often used by multiple gang members to establish status, seek revenge and even used to lure rival gang members in honey traps.

Although criminal street gangs are predominately male only, there are some girl-only street gangs operating in the UK too.

If involved with a criminal street gang it can be very difficult for members to leave. There are many organisations that can help and support young people with gang exit strategies.

Information obtained from youth charity Fearless.org www.fearless.org

Fearless.org is the youth service of Crimestoppers charity and works to empower young people to make informed decisions about reporting crime. The website www.fearless.org allows young people to access non-judgemental information and advice about crime, and also offers a safe place to give information about crime 100% anonymously. In addition to our website, Fearless also runs workshops in schools and for community youth groups, as well as providing training to youth professionals. Please contact the Fearless Team directly (fearless@crimestoppers-uk.org) to find out if there is a Fearless Outreach Worker in your area delivering these sessions. You can also request posters highlighting Fearless and their anonymous reporting service, for free, via their website.

www.fearless.org

How many children are in gangs? The data's not good enough to know

In brief.

By Joël Reland

Claim

More than 30,000 children aged between 10 and 15 now say they are in gangs.

'More than 30,000 children aged between 10 and 15 now say that they are in gangs, according to research that will fuel concerns about the country's violent crime epidemic.'

– *The Times*, 25 June 2018

The 30,000 estimate has significant limitations, and cannot be fairly used to draw a link to a supposed rising crime epidemic.

The figure of 30,000 children comes from the Office of the Children's Commissioner. It produced this estimate in a 2017 study, using data from 2013/14 from the Office for National Statistics (ONS), which reported that 0.9% of 10–15-year-olds it surveyed in England and Wales described themselves as being in a street gang.

But this figure is subject to significant uncertainty, as the Office of the Children's Commissioner noted at the time. The survey didn't include children who are detained, 'missing', or living in health and care residential establishments, and the definition of a street gang is quite broad.

The figure of 30,000 could vary a lot if there's just a small amount of error in the survey's findings. The 0.9% figure equates to about 26 young people (in a survey of 3,000) reporting themselves as being in a gang. In a repeat survey for 2016/17, it found 0.7% did so, but that's the equivalent of about five fewer young people.

Ultimately, the sample size, infrequency and wider data-recording issues mean we can't confidently say exactly how many children are in gangs, and whether this number has gone up or down in recent years. While this is the best available data we have on gangs, it cannot be taken as evidence that young people are fuelling a 'violent crime epidemic'.

This article does not assess whether or not there is such an 'epidemic'.

The 30,000 estimate comes from 2014

0.9% of 10–15-year-olds in England in Wales reported that they were a member of a street gang, according to ONS data for 2013/14, sourced to the Crime Survey for England and Wales. This is the data which *The Times* report says the Office of the Children's Commissioner used.

In 2017, the Office of the Children's Commissioner used the 0.9% figure to estimate that around 30,000 10–15-year-olds were in street gangs in England, based on population figures for England (mid-2015). It also assumes that gang-membership levels are the same in both England and Wales.

The ONS published more recent data in May this year (which wouldn't have been available to the Children's Commissioner when their report was published). It finds that 0.7% of 10–15-year-olds in England and Wales reported being in a gang in 2016/17. It also reports that 0.2% of 16–24-year-olds are a member of a street gang, compared to 0.7% in the 2013/14 data.

The data can't give us a very precise number

The sample sizes of the research mean it's hard to precisely estimate the number of children in gangs, or change over time. Applying the reported percentage of 10–15-year-olds in gangs to population statistics suggests that the number in England has fallen by 7,000 from 2013/14 to 2016/17.

This data cannot be treated as evidence for a supposed violent crime epidemic

The lack of consistently published data and limitations in recording practices mean it's hard to get a perfect picture around the number of young people in gangs. It certainly seems a stretch to use the existing data as evidence of a phenomenon which is fuelling a supposed 'violent crime epidemic', given the limitations we highlight above.

Yet this is the equivalent to about five fewer people (in a survey of around 3,000) reporting that they are in a gang in the 2016/17 survey. Given what we also know about young children responding inaccurately, or giving 'funny' answers, in surveys, this data isn't good enough to give a very precise sense of change over time.

Street gangs are also not necessarily committing criminal activities, according to the ONS definition. It told us its survey defined a street gang as:

'groups of young people who hang around together and

- have a specific area or territory;
- have a name, a colour or something else to identify the group;
- possibly have rules or a leader; or
- who may commit crimes together.'

There are more reasons these numbers should be treated with caution

The 30,000 figure formed part of a report on vulnerable children, in which the Children's Commissioner recognised that the data available to it on street gangs was limited and 'should be treated with caution'. It added: 'The information for people involved in gangs or have been victims of gangs is very limited and our research revealed an important gap in the data.'

It also highlighted that the ONS data doesn't cover 'people living in health and care residential establishments as well as people detained are not included in these estimates. Children included in the missing population may face an increased risk to be involved in gangs and thus the estimates may underreport the real numbers.'

The Office of the Children's Commissioner told us that: 'We don't collect data but collate it from many sources and sometimes the starting point for an estimate may be, in our own view, statistically dated, or weak but nonetheless, within certain standards, the best available at the time. Where that is the case we do what we think we can, transparently, to model towards a reasonable estimate of what the number is at the time of publishing.'

The Office of the Children's Commissioner told us that: 'Ever since the Office of the Children's Commissioner undertook to assess the levels of vulnerable children in England in 2016, with a view to publishing findings in 2017, there has been a dual purpose.

'Firstly to fill an existing statistical gap and find the best possible and reliable estimates we could for numbers that previously have not been calculated, and to beg the question "why hadn't they been?" ...

'Secondly to highlight how hard it can be to arrive at those numbers when data collection can be patchy, sometimes non-existent, subject to local variation, variations of interpretation of official terms (not least the word "vulnerable") and in what form the data came.'

They also said that: 'In looking to next year part of our call on government and local authorities and other services will be to provide our calculations on vulnerable children with data that is fresher, more robust and comprehensive on the area of gang membership.'

28 June 2018

Conclusion

We don't know the exact number, and it's difficult to get an accurate measure of this. In 2013/14, a survey found 0.9% of 10–15-year-olds in England and Wales said they were in a street gang, which implies around 30,000 children in England, but this should not be taken as exact.

The 40 crimes you've almost definitely committed

YouGov predicts we're stealing £4.2 million worth of plastic bags a year.

By James Rodger

Three-quarters of British residents admit to committing tiny crimes, according to a new survey.

The new study has revealed a microcrime wave is sweeping the UK – but are you a part of it?

Pollsters YouGov have found that 74 per cent of British people are 'micro-criminals'.

The most commonly committed micro-crime is paying someone cash-in-hand knowing that they won't pay tax, with 43 per cent of us confessing to this micro-crime.

After this, the next most commonly committed micro-crimes were illegally streaming (28 per cent) and downloading (25 per cent) TV shows, movies or music.

Supermarkets can rest assured that their self-service checkouts aren't a beacon for criminals as the least commonly committed micro-crime on the list was putting a product through on a self-service till for less than it should actually cost, with just nine per cent of people admitting to this – and only one per cent saying they did it frequently.

The loss of plastic bags should be of more concern to the supermarkets, with 17 per cent of people saying they have taken a plastic bag without paying for it.

YouGov predicts we're stealing £4.2 million worth of plastic bags a year.

West Midlands Police say that many of these crimes would go unpunished as they aren't often reported to them.

Top 40 'small' laws

1. Drank alcohol under the age of 18
2. Sworn or gestured to other road users
3. Eaten or drank whilst driving
4. Vacuumed between the hours of 6pm & 8am on a weekday or 1pm & 8am on a Saturday or on a Sunday
5. Parked partly on a payment
6. Cycled on pavements
7. Speeding whilst driving
8. Pocketed change when given wrong amount
9. Beeped a horn for any reason other than alerting traffic

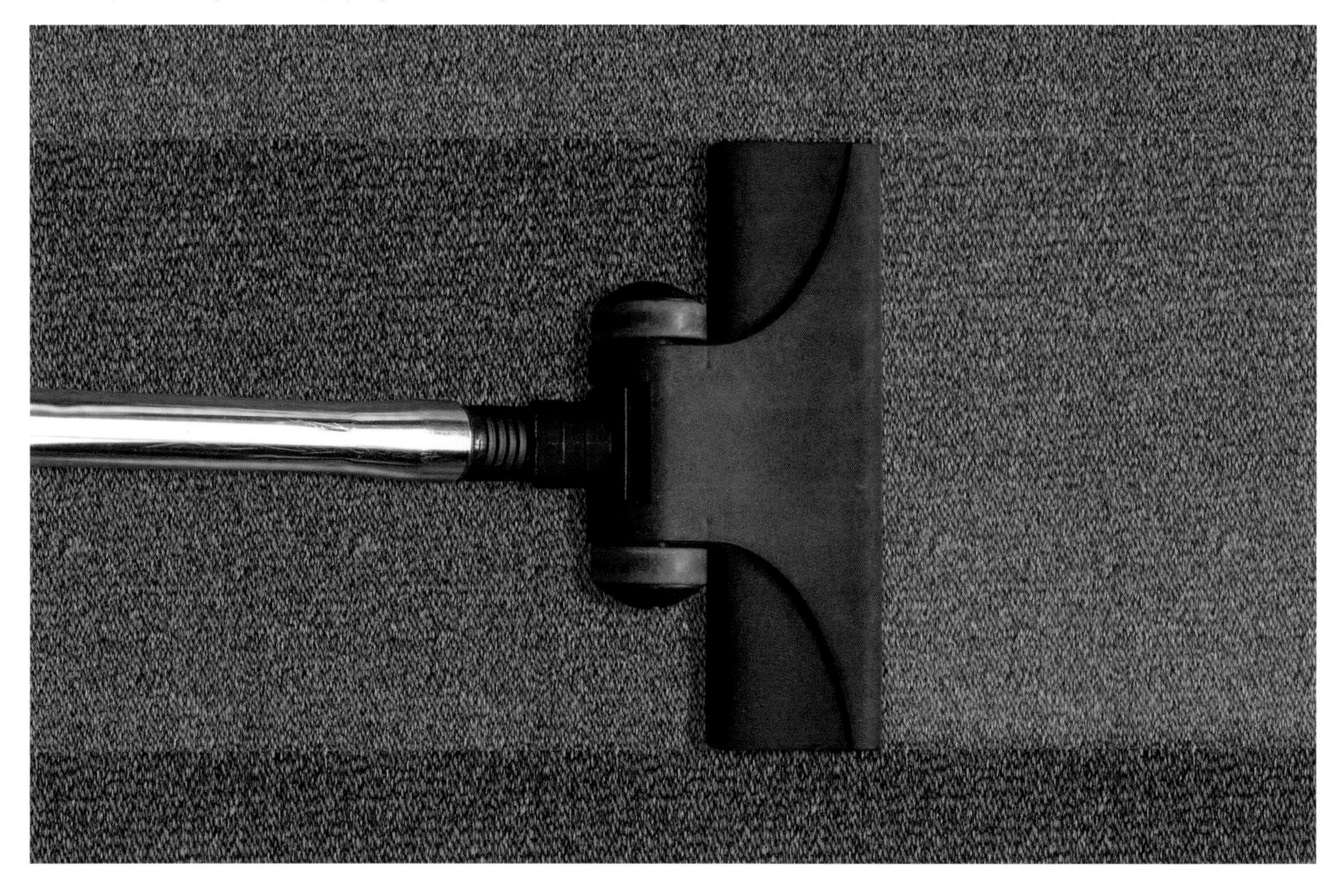

10. Been drunk on the street, in a pub or in a restaurant
11. Changed a CD whilst driving
12. Had sex in a public place
13. Bought cigarettes under the age of 18
14. Dropped litter
15. Taken illegal drugs
16. Disturbed people by ringing their doorbells/ knocking at their doors and leaving before being answered (or playing knock, knock, ginger – also known as knock down ginger)
17. Not worn a seatbelt during a car journey
18. Flown a kite in a park
19. Used a fake name on the internet
20. Stuck a postage stamp upside down
21. Used a mobile phone while driving
22. Cycled without lights after dark
23. Parked on double yellow lines
24. Driven through a red light
25. Not paid for a carrier bag at a self-service check-out
26. Had sex when you were under 16 years of age
27. Not had a TV licence and watched TV

28. Used someone else's Wi-Fi without them knowing
29. Smoked in a non-smoking area
30. Thrown tree cuttings back over your neighbours' garden
31. Claimed an item at the self-service till without paying for it
32. Taken a child out of school for a holiday – without the head teacher's permission
33. Not informed the DVLA of a change of name or address
34. Not cleaned up after your dog has pooed on the street/public path
35. Cycled through a red light
36. Fiddled your expenses
37. Sung or chanted a crude football chant in the street
38. Gone fishing without a licence
39. Parked opposite a junction
40. Put make-up on while driving.

29 July 2017

Knife crime in England and Wales

House of Commons Library briefing paper number SN4304.

By Grahame Allen, Lukas Audickas, Philip Loft, Alexander Bellis

Summary

Recorded crime

In the year ending March 2019, there were around 47,000 (selected) offences involving a knife or sharp instrument in England and Wales. Recent trends in offences have been affected by undercounting in the Greater Manchester Police Force area prior to 2018/19. Excluding or including figures from Greater Manchester, this is the highest number of offences since the year ending March 2011, the earliest point at which comparable data are available.[1] This is directly related with improvements in recording practices.[2]

Homicide

In the year ending March 2018 there were 285 homicides (currently recorded) using a sharp instrument, including knives and broken bottles, accounting for 39% of all homicides – a rise from the 212 recorded in the year ending March 2017.[3]

Knife crime by police force area

London recorded the highest rate of 169 offences involving a knife per 100,000 population in 2018/19, a slight increase on a rate of 167 in 2017/18.[4] Gwent had the lowest rate of 24 offences per 100,000 individuals (up from 19 in 2017/18).

Proven offences and offenders

In the year ending March 2019, there were 22,041 disposals given for possession of a knife or offensive weapon. Juveniles (aged 10–17) were the offenders in 21% of cases.

Hospital admissions

There were 5,149 finished consultant episodes (FCE) recorded in English hospitals in 2018/19 due to assault by a sharp object. This was an increase of nearly 2% compared to 2017/18 and 41% higher than in 2014/15

30 September 2019

1 ONS, Crime in England and Wales: Police Recorded Crime, 18 July 2019.
2 ONS, Crime in England and Wales: Police Recorded Crime, 18 July 2019.
3 ONS, Homicide in England and Wales: Year ending March 2018, 7 February 2019.
4 Metropolitan and City of London police forces combined.

www.parliament.uk

Knife crime highest recorded level in 9 years

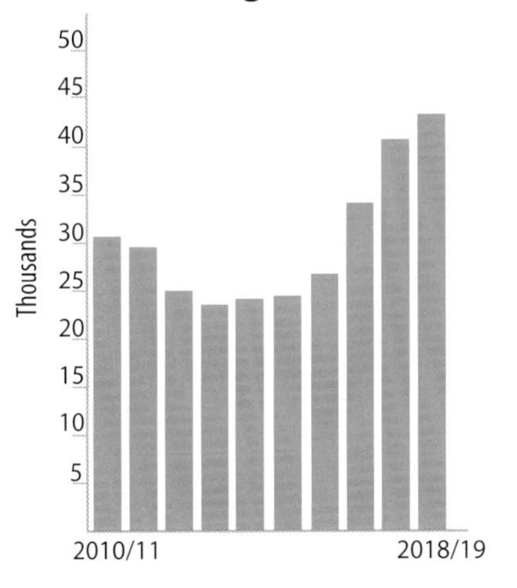

Highest/lowest rate of offences involving a sharp instrument 2018/2019 (per 100,000 population)

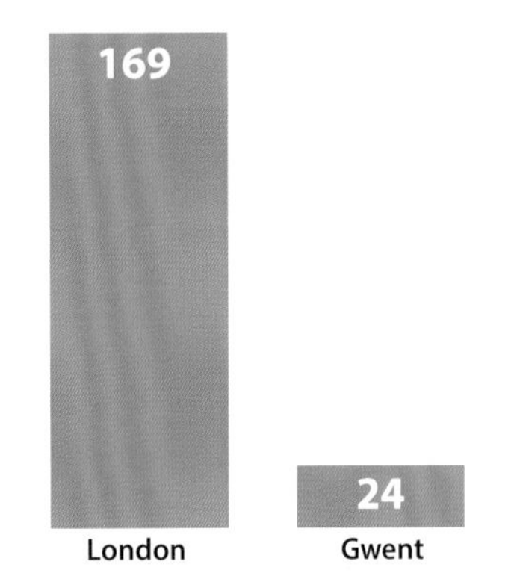

Hospital episodes[1] since 1998/99[2]

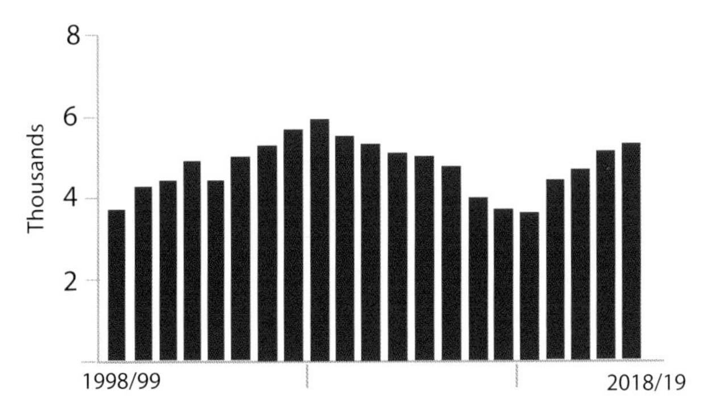

1. Finished consultant episode (FCE).
2. In 2014/15 the lowest number since 1998/9 was recorded.

Knife crime

Knife crime is devastating for victims their family and the wider community. Knife attacks involving young people hit the headlines too frequently.

Effects of knife crime

Social

Reports of stabbings in the news increase the fear and worry in the community. Some young people may feel that if other young people are carrying knives, they should be doing the same and carrying a knife for protection. More knives on the street only leads to one outcome – more people getting hurt.

Physical

If you are stabbed, the wound and trauma to the body could tragically result in death. Although some people believe there are 'safe' areas of the body to stab this isn't true. You have arteries which carry your precious blood all over your body. So a stab wound in the legs and arms should be treated as seriously as those in the neck or chest.

If you are stabbed and survive you could still experience long-term physical effects. If you look at a stab wound it is usually a short wound on the surface of the skin - but very deep in your body, this will of course vary depending on the type of weapon used. This type of internal wound means that the affected area may be prone to infection and as a result never heal properly.

Ask yourself a question – Will the person who stabbed you have made sure their knife was clean and bacteria free? Not very nice but hopefully you get the idea.

Physiological

- As a victim. If you survive being stabbed you will have still experienced major trauma to your body. It is likely to take you a long time to heal. You might find it difficult going out on your own as you are frightened you might be attacked again. You survived and experienced a nasty crime and you may have bad dreams reliving what happened to you. It is likely to have an impact on your family and friends who will be worried for you. If you have been a victim of a crime please visit Victim Support for help and support.
- As the offender. If you really had the intention to stab and kill someone you may feel happy when you find out your victim has died. In reality this is not often the case. How do you think you will really feel? How will your family feel about what you have done? You are very likely to get caught, so will face a long time in prison. Are you ready and prepared to do this? These may be questions that you will have to answer if you do get charged with murder. Only you know the right answers.

DID YOU KNOW?

It is illegal to sell a knife to anybody under the age of 18

Knife crime includes any crimes that involve the use of a sharpened weapon, blade or offensive weapon. The way these types of weapons can be used means there are a number of different types of knife crime.

There are also certain knives that are banned in the UK, meaning you could be arrested and charged simply for owning one. These include: flick knives, butterfly knives, disguised knives, sword-sticks and gravity knives.

Two strikes rule. If you have been caught before with a knife, you could risk a more severe punishment if you are caught again. In a new law that was passed on 17 July 2015, if you are aged between 12 and 17 years and are caught twice with a knife, you are likely to face at least a four months detention and training order.

Knives are the most common weapons used in the killings of young people and if someone is injured or killed in your presence you could be sent to prison for murder or attempted murder under 'joint enterprise'.

Information obtained from youth charity Fearless.org www.fearless.org

Fearless.org is the youth service of Crimestoppers charity and works to empower young people to make informed decisions about reporting crime. The website www.fearless.org allows young people to access non-judgemental information and advice about crime, and also offers a safe place to give information about crime 100% anonymously. In addition to their website, Fearless also runs workshops in schools and for community youth groups, as well as providing training to youth professionals. Please contact the Fearless Team directly (fearless@crimestoppers-uk.org) to find out if there is a Fearless Outreach Worker in your area delivering these sessions. You can also request posters highlighting Fearless and their anonymous reporting service, for free, via their website.

www.fearless.org

SHARP FACTS

1. Possession of a knife carries a prison sentence of up to four years even if it's not used.
2. If you are caught with a knife it doesn't matter if it was for your own protection or you were carrying it for someone else – you will be arrested and prosecuted. Self-protection is not a reasonable excuse for carrying an offensive weapon.
3. The legal definition of an offensive weapon includes anything intended to be used to harm another person, like a sharpened comb. It's also illegal to carry a 'disguised knife' – anything with a concealed blade or sharp point that's made to look like an everyday object (like a pen, cigarette lighter or lipstick).
4. There is no 'safe place' to stab someone. Get stabbed in the heart and you can loose all of your blood in one minute. But a wound in the arm or the leg can still kill and young people have died from wounds to the leg because an artery was severed.
5. Knife crime can affect anyone, not just people in gangs. Innocent bystanders can get caught in the middle of other people's disputes and suffer trauma, serious injuries or worse.
6. Knife crime is falling in Scotland, fewer people are carrying knives and doing so is becoming less and less acceptable among young people.
7. Police can – and do – stop and search anyone they think is carrying a weapon.
8. It's illegal to carry a knife or offensive weapon in a public place without a reasonable excuse. Reasonable excuses include those who need them for work, like fishermen or carpet fitters, but this only applies while they're actually at work.
9. If you stab somebody and they die, you'll face a life sentence and serve a minimum of 25 years.
10. Even if it's not you who does it, if someone is injured or killed by a knife in your presence you could be sent to prison for murder or attempted murder in what is referred to as 'joint enterprise'.
11. It's illegal for shops to sell knives to anyone under 18 and buying a knife under the age of 18 is an offence. This includes kitchen knives and even cutlery.
12. By carrying a knife, you are much more likely to get stabbed yourself as situations involving weapons can quickly get out of control.
13. Knives are the most common weapons used in killings of young people.
14. If you have a criminal record you might not be accepted into a college or university, get a job, or travel to some countries, like the USA, Canada or Australia.

5 September 2018

For more information and advice visit:
www.noknivesbetterlives.com

www.noknivesbetterlives.com

'Like fires everywhere': West Midlands becomes a youth knife-crime hotspot

The causes are numerous and complex, but it is the scale and the age of those involved that alarms adults on the frontline.

By Ben Quinn

With a metallic creak, the door to one of Birmingham's 'weapons surrender bins' opened to reveal a plethora of blades, from kitchen knives to karambits, claw-shaped knives commonly used in south-east Asian martial arts which have lately featured in some computer games.

It was a collection that had been building in the windswept car park of a church in the Hockley area of the city before being unlocked last week.

Despite being dismissed by some as a PR stunt, the container is one of a network of 12 in the West Midlands that is be expanded as part of a range of measures in a region that has experienced the biggest increase in knife crime outside of London.

The fatal stabbing in Coventry on Saturday of 16-year-old Jaydon Washington James – killed, according to his sister, because of his postcode – brought the number of teenagers and younger children killed by knives in the West Midlands police force area to six this year, more per capita than in London and a 40-year high.

A previous spike came in 2013 when four people under-20 were fatally stabbed.

The five of those killed so far this year were from a black and minority ethnic background, the youngest 8 and 11.

'We are alarmed by the sheer number and we are alarmed by the ages of those involved,' said Katie Wright, an A&E consultant and co-lead of children's emergency department at Birmingham's Heartlands hospital, as she gestured towards an entrance door where people who have been stabbed are regularly dumped by those who would prefer not to attract the police attention that comes with calling for an ambulance.

Recent patients have included an 11-year-old who has been carrying a knife because he felt unsafe in his area, says Wright. She added that Heartlands' location in an area with 'massive' levels of deprivation resulted in minors frequently coming to A&E because of alcohol and drug problems, events at home and self-harm.

'Very often they are the ones who we see further down the line presenting with stab injuries,' said Wright, who likened the violence to a contagious disease that should be treated as a public health problem.

Chest, back and face wounds account for the vast majority of cases – sometimes seemingly carried out because of myths about those parts of the body being non-fatal places to stab – although medics also see life-changing abdominal wounds.

Like others working on the frontline of dealing with knife crime in the West Midlands, Wright was quick to point to poverty as one of the factors behind the rise.

Although a landmark 2017 report on gangs and violence in the West Midlands concluded it was difficult to explain the increase in both gun and knife crimes in recent years, it listed a mosaic of reasons cited by police, community groups, former gang members and others.

They included the emergences of a 'new generation of gangsters' known for spontaneous acts of violence, the role of social media and music, mental health issues and what some referred to as the 'father deficit'. Above all, perhaps, there was the impact of government austerity measures that resulted in the West Midlands experiencing some the steepest cuts in funding for youth work.

In Wolverhampton, the budget for youth services shrank by 86% between 2014–2017. Catch22 is a youth organisation that runs a 'violence reduction team' aimed at supporting and rehabilitating young people inside or on the fringes of gangs. Its caseworkers said it has had a dramatic increase in referrals in the past 18 months, with the youngest person it recently helped being only seven years old.

Funded from the budget of the West Midlands police and crime commissioner (PCC), the team's three caseworkers are working with 80 young people but could easily double that, given the right resources.

Out of a group of five of its young clients who answered questions from *The Guardian* passed on by Catch22, four said they carry or had carried a knife.

One, who carried a knife for protection, said: 'You could probably try and calm the situation in some areas, but in other areas it isn't possible, because people are revenging what's already happened.'

Another said: 'I don't carry a knife, but, yes, someone's tried to stab me. We need youth clubs, in every area.'

Former gang members who now mentor the young express surprise that carrying a knife has become common place among a new generation. Two mentors, who work in different parts of the West Midlands, spoke of a 'desensitisation' towards violence, in some cases citing the role of computer games. They also emphasised deprivation as a factor and one over-riding catalyst: fear.

'It's the age of people who are involved which is the biggest shock to me,' said James Gwilt, who served a prison sentence for arms offences. He compared his mentoring of at-risk young people to feeling like he was 'continually trying to extinguish fires popping up everywhere'.

Gwilt adds: 'Families are fracturing. Poverty has always been here but now it really feels like a generation are having upbringings without any love. When me and my friends were in that life we still had good upbringings. Nan was in the kitchen preparing a meal. Now she's probably on Facebook.'

Simeon Moore was once affiliated to a Birmingham gang known as the Johnson Crew. He bemoaned the absence of more male mentors from communities affected by knife crime and the lack of backing.

'It's also about the aunties, the uncles, the cousins. We literally need teams of people out on the streets and in the schools,' he said.

Moore's words echoed one of the key criticisms of the 2017 report on gangs and violence in the region. It said there were no examples of genuine 'power-sharing' between communities and the statutory, private and voluntary sectors in the West Midlands.

The office of David Jamieson, the PCC for the West Midlands, said community organisations were included in an implementation group overseeing a raft of initiatives ranging from the knife bins to funding for campaigns in schools. His office also part-funds Redthread's youth violence intervention programme in collaboration with doctors such as Wright. The pilot scheme places youth workers in A&E departments across the Midlands to provide 'tailored' support for young people at risk of youth violence or exploitation.

Police cuts are cited as one of the backdrops to the rise in violent crime by Jamieson and Pat McFadden, one of a number of Midlands MPs who have been pressing the Home Office on the issue and led a Commons debate on the matter this month. West Midlands police has lost a quarter of its officers (about 2,000) in recent years.

Both also point to local authorities cuts that have led to the provision of youth services in the West Midlands coming to, in Jamieson's words, a standstill.

Another factor is causing particular concern to Jamieson: the 'off-rolling' of pupils by schools, which he said was deliberate in order to enhance overall exam results.

'These are very often the children who find themselves involved in knife-related crime. Some of the nastiest episodes we have seen have almost always involved children from this group. They are being failed by some of the very institutions that are supposed to be one of their first and foremost supports,' Jamieson added.

Det Supt Ian Parnell is the West Midlands police's lead officer on knife crime. He said the force was recording between 250 and 280 knife-related offences a month and that this had followed a 'worrying' increase in recent years.

'It's incredibly complex as you don't have one particular crime you can focus on,' said Parnell. 'It might be related to gang issues, school issues, the night-time economy or domestic violence. It also tends to involve young males of all races and backgrounds, so it's difficult to tailor a response to such a broad spectrum of people.'

While focused on 'listening' to young people, he said stop and search had a role, provided it was based on firm intelligence and in consultation with communities. He said the West Midlands was in a good position on this, there was still a 'battle' about the tactic's future.

He added: 'One idea I would like to explore is around 'safe routes'. What can we do in partnership with the community and schools to reduce the fear and reduce after school violence and the propensity to carry knives.'

29 November 2018

www.theguardian.com

Knife crime soars in rural areas by as much as 50 per cent as violence epidemic spreads out of cities

By Charles Hymas and Patrick Scott

Knife crime rose by up to 50 per cent in rural areas in the past year as violence spread from cities, fuelled by county lines drug gangs, official figures show.

Suffolk, Norfolk, North Yorkshire, Derbyshire, Kent, Lancashire and Dyfed-Powys saw some of the biggest rises as knife crime overall in England and Wales rose by eight per cent to 43,516 offences, its highest since records began eight years ago.

At the same time, the proportion of crimes solved has fallen by half in four years, with fewer than one in 12 offences (7.8 per cent) resulting in a charge or summons. That is a fall from 9.1 per cent last year and 15 per cent four years ago.

Policing minister Nick Hurd admitted: 'We are deeply concerned that certain offences, including serious violence, have increased and we are taking urgent action.'

Robbery rose by 11 per cent to 85,700 offences, the number of killings increased from 693 to 701, violence against people was up 20 per cent to almost 1.7 million offences and sex crimes including rape were up by seven per cent to 162,000.

The overall crime rate rose by eight per cent to 5.95 million offences for the year ending March 2019, according to the Office for National Statistics (ONS).

Boris Johnson, the Tory leadership frontrunner, and Sajid Javid, the Home Secretary, have pledged to reverse police cuts by recruiting an extra 20,000 officers and have backed greater use of stop-and-search to combat the knife crime epidemic.

County lines gangs, who run drugs out of cities into local communities, are blamed for the rise in rural knife crime, with Suffolk up 51.4 per cent to 221 offences, Dyfed-Powys up by 44.9 per cent to 229 and Lancashire up by 32.8 per cent to 1,151.

In North Yorkshire, it increased by 31 per cent to 300, in Norfolk, it was up 27.7 per cent to 281, in Gwent by 25.9 per cent to 141, Derbyshire 23.5 per cent to 610 and Kent up 20.4 per cent to 955.

Two big cities also saw big rises in knife crime with Merseyside up 48.6 per cent to 1,404 and West Midlands up 48.6 per cent to 1,404.

By contrast, the Metropolitan police, which has surged officers onto the streets and dramatically increased use of stop-and-search slowed the rise in knife crime to just 0.9 per cent with 14,842 offences.

Sarah Jones, chair of the all party knife crime group, said: 'Today's figures show the Government has been far too slow to tackle county lines activity which sees vulnerable, armed young people trafficked into towns across our country.'

Offences involving firearms also rose by three per cent to 6,684. Theft offences remained static, at just over two million with burglary down by three per cent to 422,870 offences. Drug offences were up by 11 per cent to 151,500, while fraud and computer misuse crimes rose by nine per cent to 693,418.

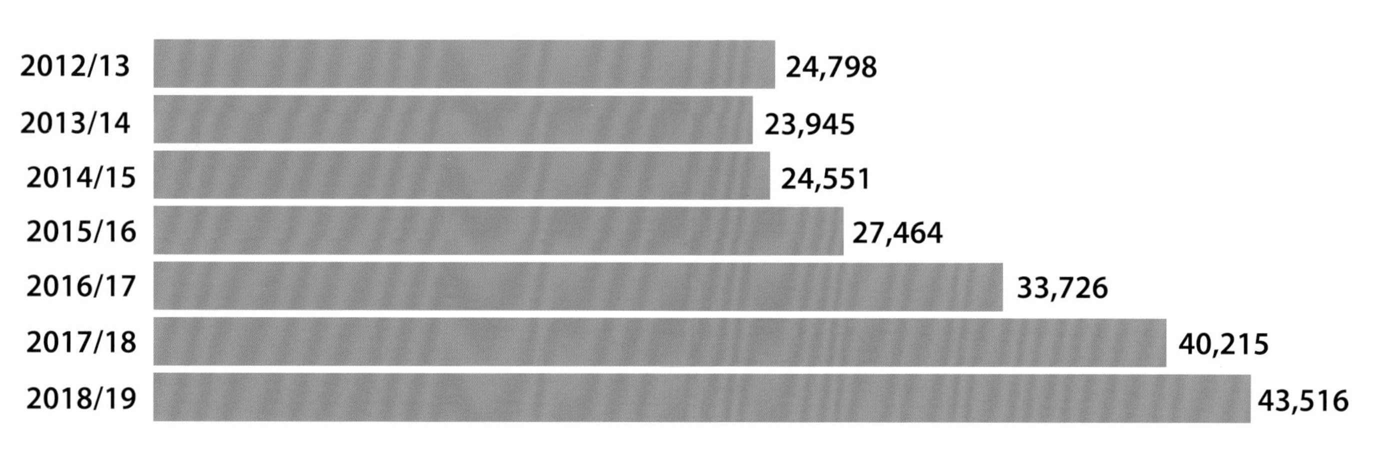

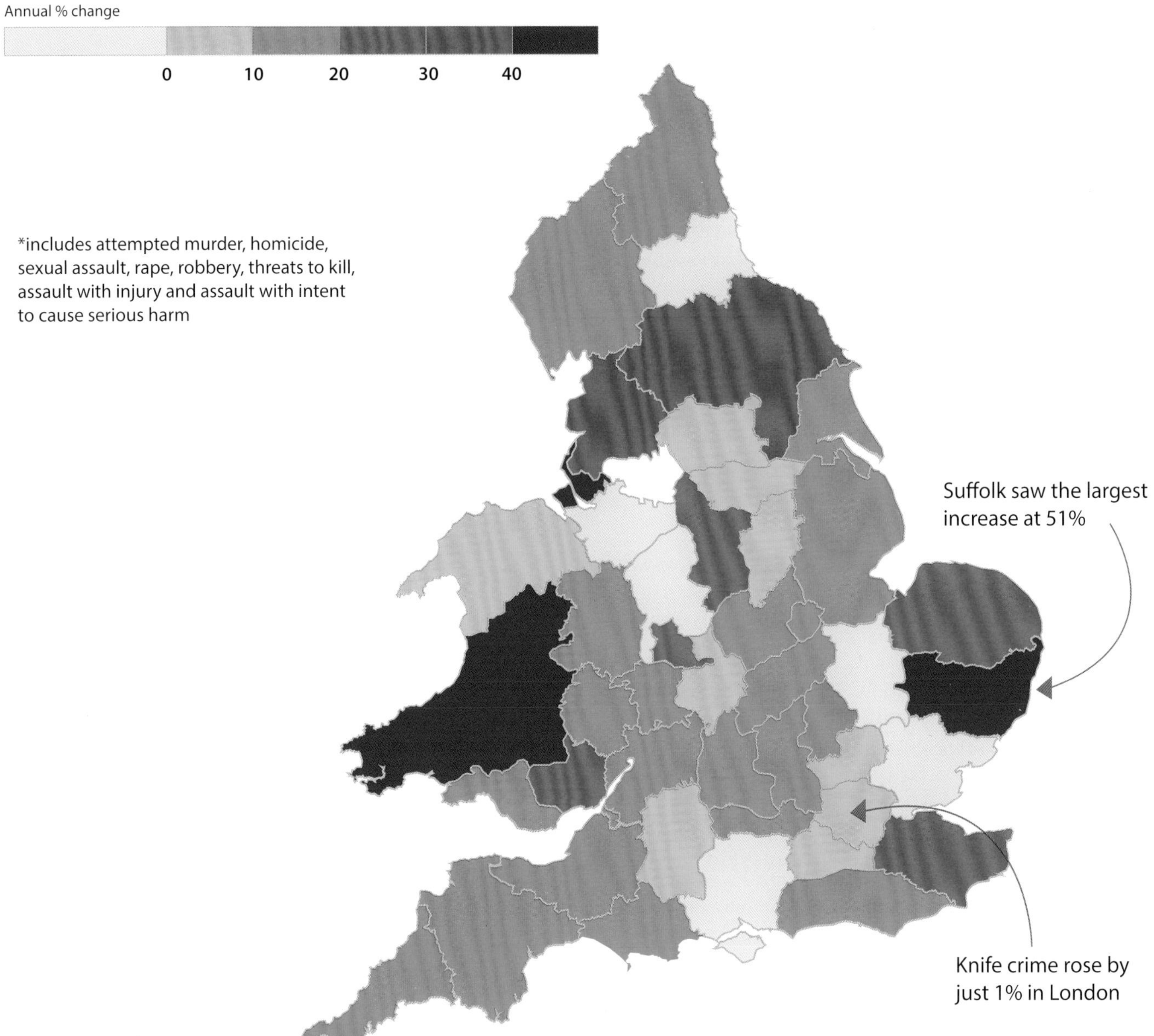

The total number of offences solved fell by 39,496 with the proportion resulting in a charge or summons down from 9.1 per cent to 7.8 per cent.

Sex offences were least likely to be solved at 3.5 per cent followed by theft at 5.7 per cent, criminal damage and arson at 5.3 per cent, robbery at 7.4 per cent and violence against the person at 8.3 per cent.

The proportion of offences that were closed as a result of 'evidential difficulties' increased from 29 per cent to 32 per cent.

Police forces closed almost half (44 per cent) of offences with no suspect identified, a similar proportion to last year.

This proportion varied by crime type with around 74 per cent of theft offences closed in this way compared with nine per cent of rape offences and two per cent of drugs offences.

Javed Khan, chief executive of Barnardo's, Britain's biggest children's charity, said: "It's unacceptable that the knife crime crisis continues unabated with offences at record levels.

'Children are not born with knives in their hands, knife crime is a symptom of a much bigger problem. Our frontline support services say vulnerable children and young people are being recruited and exploited by criminal gangs and forced to traffic drugs and carry knives.

'Urgent action must be taken so that future generations are not condemned to live in an endless spiral of violence.'

8 August 2019

www.telegraph.co.uk

Knife crime statistics: rates rising higher in Manchester, Liverpool and Slough than in some London boroughs

London remains the most dangerous place overall in relation to knife crime, however.

By Serina Sandhu

The rate of serious knife crime in places such as Manchester, Liverpool, Slough and Blackpool is higher than in some London boroughs, it has been reported.

Dispelling the myth that the issue of knife attacks is confined to London, the BBC said there had been a sharp increase in offences outside the capital.

The report follows Donald Trump's repeated critiques of Mayor of London Sadiq Khan over violent crime, including calling him 'a national disgrace who is destroying' the capital.

However, the BBC's analysis of police figures also showed London, which had 16 of the top 25 areas for knife crime (more than one crime per 10,000 people), was still more dangerous than other cities.

According to the corporation's Freedom of Information responses from 34 of England and Wales' 43 police forces, in Manchester there were 24.6 knife crimes per 10,000 people between 2016 and 2018. For Liverpool, Slough and Blackpool it was 16.3, 15.6 and 14.3 per 10,000 people, respectively.

'Small cities get no mention'

Knife crime grew 1.7 times in Preston between 2016 and 2018, and 1.6 times in both Stoke-on-Trent and Bedford.

Byron Highton, whose brother was 18 when he was stabbed to death with a sword and an axe in Preston five years ago, said the whole country was suffering from knife crime but 'small cities in the north like Preston get no mention'.

He told the BBC: 'Young people have a lack of respect for life. The scary part is how bad is it going to be in 10 years if this generation isn't fixed.'

Sajda Mughal OBE, CEO of the Jan Trust which runs programmes to tackle knife crime, told *i*: 'As the number of young people living in poverty up and down the country grows, more and more are pushed into finding ways to support their families and themselves financially. They are forced as a result of the deprivation they suffer to find a way to earn money.

'The way to earn fast cash can result in young people becoming involved with drugs and therefore knives. Tackling this growth means we need to invest in young people's futures and provide them with viable and meaningful opportunities and the services that allow them to flourish,' she added.

In the London boroughs of Tower Hamlets, Haringey and Hackney knife crime grew 1.3 times. In Newham, the rate of knife crime stayed the same – at 19.1 per 10,000 people – between 2016 and 2018.

Among the safest places in England and Wales were Dorset and the Cotswolds.

'We're taking action'

Commenting on the BBC report, the Home Office said: "We are taking action to tackle the violent crime which has such a devastating impact on our communities.

'This includes supporting the police by recruiting 20,000 new police officers over the next three years, making it easier for them to use stop and search powers, and investing £10 million in additional funding to allow forces to increase the number of officers carrying Tasers.

'This week the Home Secretary announced an additional £20 million to tackle county lines, including expanding the National County Lines Co-ordination Centre.'

7 October 2019

Police won't solve the knife crime epidemic – but community work can

THE CONVERSATION

An article from The Conversation.

Helen Millward, Teaching Fellow in Marketing, Keele University

Knife crime is a growing concern in England and Wales, with the UK Government pledging an additional £100 million to tackle what West Midlands Police have named a 'national emergency'. Figures show that the number of knife crime incidents is rising. In England, there were 5,053 knife assaults recorded in 2017–18, an increase of 14% since 2016–17 and 39% higher than in 2014–15. Just over one in five knife offenders are between the ages of 10 and 17.

Recent media focus has suggested that budgetary cuts and the fall in police officer numbers are to blame. Commentators also question the long-term efficacy of preventive methods such as police stop and search powers, mediation and test-purchasing of weapons in shops, ensuring only those 18 or older are able to buy weapons.

Worryingly, research points to a close correlation between knife crime and a raft of social problems such as poverty, school exclusions, ill mental health and rising numbers of children with complex needs and vulnerabilities. But it is hard to say how these factors relate to each other and whether they cause – or are caused by – knife crime.

The recent increase in budget to tackle knife crime indicates that the issue is being taken seriously by the Government. For example, £1.5 million has been earmarked for activities such as purchasing new police cars and hand-held metal detectors, gaining new staff and mentoring programmes.

But stop and search and test-purchasing of weapons cannot address the complicated social problems that are linked to knife crime. Stop and search powers do not help to positively change an area's culture, for example. They can alienate community members and can foster feelings of mistrust and division within communities already divided by offending and anti-social behaviour.

Those living within communities where there are problems are often those best placed to understand what is going on and why. Police understand that outreach is an effective way of getting to know community members and hearing their concerns. For example, in the West Midlands, £100,000 of funding is to be given to young people to help them improve their communities 'via local initiatives'. This isn't a very large amount of funding: police budgets for outreach are under pressure and the majority of police powers only equip officers to deal with knife crime after the fact, rather than focusing on prevention.

The power of community

Community outreach involves community members coming together in attempts to tackle a shared problem, typically an issue affecting the community's local area. Community outreach groups can work in partnership with other organisations, which can often be helpful in gaining funding to further the impact of activities.

For example, a community outreach group that wants to address food poverty in their community may want to work with a local food bank, food store or university. Community

'The project was about personal choice and how things from the past don't have to haunt you, and you can change it... so you just have to be conscious make the right choice next time.'

Changing hearts and minds

Results have been positive, with particular success in supporting new social networks and connections. One elderly lady who participated in an outreach workshop said that she was initially quite wary of young offenders within the community, for example, but this changed when she met some of the people in question at a workshop. She realised they were not 'thuggish, they were just kids'.

The degree of reflection was also noted among ex-offenders. Some even came forward to volunteer at the theatre after the project finished. Practitioners realised that some of the ex-offenders had gained 'the confidence to go back into education' or to feel 'confident enough to apply for a job and start working'. This suggests that these people are less likely to offend again and are increasing their capacity to make positive social and cultural contributions.

outreach sees residents as a part of the solution to social problems and encourages proactive behaviour, rather than passively waiting for issues to be solved by, for example, the police or government departments.

Our research explores new techniques of community outreach undertaken in partnership with a local theatre in a deprived area of the West Midlands, UK. Here the police were not leading the workshops: instead they were facilitated by theatre practitioners. A variety of creative methods, including poetry, craft and drama, helped to tailor activities to those in attendance.

We attended the workshops and participated with the aim of gaining an understanding of the issues facing the local area, as seen by community members themselves. The creative methods used at the workshops helped us to understand a variety of issues such as local crime, to get to know those affected and to build better relations between community members. Longer term, the aim was to kindle trust, reduce fear and tackle some of the underlying social disadvantages which can lead to offending.

At the heart of these workshops is the concept of co-creation and its core principle of social equality. The practical effect of this is to remove issues of hierarchy and promote discussion between practitioners, academics and community members.

During the workshops all participate in planning and choosing approaches and feel equal ownership of the process. Nobody is the 'expert'. The activities are 'fun'– usually organised around a practical process such as craft – and serious issues only emerge when participants feel they should. These are not focus groups and because of that, we have noted little tension or confrontation. Instead, we think that reflections and ideas develop naturally. As one theatre practitioner noted:

There is also potential for these changes in attitude to generate community-wide impact because, as one of the workshop leaders explained:

'If you change one individual and they get the opportunity to change another individual then it spreads throughout their group... slowly you spread the word, whole group change is quite a big thing.'

These results are promising within the context of knife crime, particularly as it seems increasingly out of police control. At the very least, our work shows that community outreach can make a positive contribution to tackling local issues. But further government funding would significantly benefit the impact of such creative work. This would improve the ability of communities themselves to address issues such as knife crime in their local areas, rather than relying on the methods of those who may have little understanding of the best-placed solutions to fit the local area.

23 July 2019

The power of Drill and Grime music to reduce knife crime

The genre has a bad reputation, but what if I told you this music can be used for good?

By Precious Okoye

Since 2019, the UK has witnessed increases in knife and gun crimes among young people with over 78 knife-related deaths in the capital alone. The worrying increase has led to the demonisation of these music genres, with the police and media turning their blame towards the artists as instigators of the problem. However, this is not actually the case.

UK Grime began in the early 2000s and Drill, a derivation of Grime, began growing in popularity since 2012.

These music genres have seen many artists rise to fame from very humble beginnings. What we are witnessing within these genres is the creation of a bright future for their artists. The music industry has been removing artists from the streets and encouraging them to turn their energies towards more positive directions. The music industry has even allowed artists to create opportunities for other young people like themselves. A perfect example of this can be seen through Stormzy's creation of a scholarship for young black Cambridge students.

However, one must discuss the circulations of some Drill songs and artists who have been linked to actual violence. The main case highlighted by the public and used to demonise the genre, is that of a rapper commonly known as M-Trap – who was given a life sentence for stabbing a 15-year-old to death. However, as Drill artist DJ Bempah noted during an interview, if violence is what artists are witnessing in the environment around them, then it is what they will portray in their lyrics. Changes are needed to remove violence from the streets in order for artists to change the tone of their lyrics. Crucially, it is not the case that every artist from this genre embraces violent behaviour. However, the few that have been flagged by the media have contributed to the genre becoming blacklisted.

I say, it is about time we stop removing facilities and opportunities from our young people, especially young people of colour. Attempts to censor music whose artists are predominantly black will only create further divisions between these groups and the Government. Instead of policy-makers searching for the factors which have turned young people to the streets, resulting in a spike in youth violence, they are predictably blaming the same communities who are deeply affected by it. But what they should be doing is supporting them. It is not possible, nor is it fair for middle-class politicians to make decisions regarding working-class communities without their consultation. If done without first speaking and reaching out to these communities, without proper attention to detail, policies created may be insensitive and counterproductive.

The police's censorship of the West London Drill group 1011 has seen a rise in the popularity of their songs within

black and ethnic minority communities. Further attempts to police this genre will create a situation where the police lose all possible influence on the message being spread. Instead, Drill and Grime music should, and could, be used as an avenue to reach young people through what artists release.

An alternative proposal should be considered. We should not blame the entirety of the music genre for the spike in violence, to the extent of policing it. Politicians and police officers need to work with these artists, educating them on the impact of their lyrics on impressionable young people and bringing them on board on the campaign to reduce the violence we are witnessing on our streets. Recently, Rapper Yizzy created a music video illustrating the 'horrendous reality' of knife crime as he plays a stab victim. Yizzy's video is only one example of how artists can be used to spread a clear and impressionable message. For many young people, having their role models discourage gang mentality and violence, will have a better chance at decreasing their inclination to commit crime.

Politicians need to stop blaming and must start listening. The weapon needed to reduce violence lies in the hands of the same people they seek to censor. Grime and Drill is not the enemy and it can help in the fight against knife and gun crimes – we just need to learn how to use this genre for good.

8 August 2019

The Home Office has today launched a new advertising campaign to reduce knife crime among young people.

By using real-life stories of young people who made the decision not to carry knives, the #knifefree campaign aims to highlight the consequences of carrying a knife and to inspire young people to pursue positive alternatives.

Serious violence strategy

The campaign forms part of the Government's forthcoming Serious Violence Strategy, which will set out action to tackle serious violence by placing new emphasis on steering young people away from crime while continuing to promote the strongest possible law enforcement approach.

Home Secretary Amber Rudd said:

'The emotional stories at the heart of the new Knife Free campaign bring home in powerful fashion just what a far-reaching impact it can have on a young person's life if they make the misguided decision to carry a knife.

'I hope any young person who is seriously thinking about carrying a knife listens to what the implications can be and realises what options are available if they choose to live knife free.'

Minister for Crime, Safeguarding and Vulnerability Victoria Atkins said:

'This powerful new campaign will highlight the tragic consequences of carrying a knife and challenge the idea that young people are safer if they carry one.'

The £1.35-million campaign will use advertising on social media (Snapchat, Twitter) and digital channels (TV on demand, Spotify) to target 10- to 21-year-olds who use these platforms. A poster campaign will also be displayed in English cities where knife crime is more prevalent.

Real-life stories

The adverts feature real-life case studies who have turned their lives around after deciding to go knife free. They are based on new research commissioned for the campaign which found that showing real-life stories of young people talking about their experiences with knives resonated with the target audience.

The adverts point young people to a dedicated #knifefree website which provides advice, signposts support services and highlights activities to empower young people to change their behaviour.

Backing

When developing the campaign, the Home Office worked closely with a range of charities and knife crime victims' families to ensure their insights and expertise were reflected. John Poyton, chief executive of Redthread, said:

'It's incredibly important to make sure young people understand that violence and knife crime should not be normal.

'I'm really pleased that the new campaign puts young people and their stories at the forefront of its message, and highlights the positive choices they can make to live knife free.

'We know that policing is only one part of the solution and tackling this issue requires a public health approach and everyone in our communities working together.'

Patrick Green, chief executive of the Ben Kinsella Trust, said:

'It is vitally important that we help young people understand the dangers associated with carrying a knife. A knife won't protect you, it doesn't give you status; harming or stabbing someone isn't a trivial act.

'We need to do more to help young people understand that carrying a knife doesn't solve anything, in fact all it does is increase the likelihood that you will be imprisoned, seriously injured or murdered.

'Introducing young people to the life stories of others who have faced the same challenges but have chosen to live knife free is a powerful way to help them make more positive choices. That is why the Ben Kinsella Trust fully supports the live knife free campaign.'

Evan Jones, Head of Community Services at St Giles Trust, said:

'St Giles Trust wholeheartedly backs this campaign. Our staff see the effects of knife crime every day – from convictions for carrying a knife that can blight a career all the way through to meeting a young person who has suffered life-changing injuries as a result of an assault by a rival gang.

'Our staff work tirelessly to persuade young people there are safe alternatives to carrying a knife and that there are positive alternatives to gangs and criminality. They work on the streets, in gangs units, in schools, in regional towns and in hospitals, using their life experience to engage and support young people to make the changes that will keep them safe.'

The knife crime media campaign forms part of a wide range of measures underway to tackle knife crime. In February, the Home Office announced a new round of the knife crime community fund and increased the money available to charities to £1 million. The Government has also consulted on new laws on offensive and dangerous weapons, including banning online stores from delivering knives to residential addresses and making it an offence to possess certain weapons in private.

27 March 2018

History of the penal system

Prison is just one of a number of sanctions available to the courts to deal with those who commit criminal offences. Imprisonment today is the harshest sanction available, but this has not always been the case.

In the sixteenth and seventeenth centuries sanctions for criminal behaviour tended to be public events which were designed to shame and deter; these included the ducking stool, the pillory, whipping, branding and the stocks. At the time the sentence for many other offences was death.

Prison tended to be a place where people were held before their trial or while awaiting punishment. It was very rarely used as a punishment in its own right.

Evidence suggests that the prisons of this period were badly maintained. Men and women, boys and girls, debtors and murderers were all held together. Many people died of diseases such as gaol fever, which was a form of typhus.

The most important innovation of this period was the building of the prototype house of correction, the London Bridewell. Houses of correction were originally part of the machinery of the Poor Law, intended to instil habits of industry to petty offenders and vagrants through prison labour. By the end of this period they were absorbed into the prison system under the control of local Justices of the Peace.

Although the eighteenth century has been characterised as the era of the 'Bloody Code', there was growing opposition to the death penalty for all but the most serious crimes. It was an era of imprisonment with hard labour and of transportation.

Convicts were shipped to the British colonies like America, Australia and Van Diemen's Land (Tasmania). Prison hulks – ships anchored in the Thames, and at Portsmouth and Plymouth – were also used from 1776, where prisoners would be put to hard labour during the day and then loaded, in chains, onto the ship at night. The appalling conditions on the hulks eventually led to the end of this practice in 1857.

'Men and women, boys and girls, debtors and murderers were all held together. Many people died of diseases such as gaol fever, which was a form of typhus.'

In 1777, John Howard (namesake of the Howard League) condemned the prison system as disorganised, barbaric and filthy. He called for wide-ranging reforms including the installation of paid staff, outside inspection, a proper diet and other necessities for prisoners.

Howard was the first penal reformer, and others followed suit. Men and women in prison were separated and sanitation was improved.

In 1791, Jeremy Bentham designed the 'panopticon'. This prison design allowed a centrally placed observer to survey all the prisoners, as prison wings radiated out from this central position. Bentham's panopticon became the model for prison building for the next half century.

In 1799, the Pentitentiary Act specified that gaols should be built for one inmate per cell and operate on a silent system with continuous labour.

The first half of the nineteenth century represented a watershed in the history of state punishment. Imprisonment replaced capital punishment for most serious offences other than murder and the shaming sanctions such as the stocks were regarded as outdated.

'In 1777, John Howard condemned the prison system as disorganised, barbaric and filthy.'

The nineteenth century saw the birth of the state prison. The first national penitentiary was completed at Millbank in London, in 1816. It held 860 prisoners, kept in separate cells, although association with other prisoners was allowed during the day. Work in prison was mainly centred around simple tasks such as picking 'coir' (tarred rope) and weaving.

In 1842, Pentonville prison was built using the panopticon design; this prison is still used today. Pentonville was originally designed to hold 520 prisoners, each held in a cell measuring 13 feet long, seven feet wide and nine feet high. It operated the separate system, which was basically solitary confinement. Over the next six years, 54 new prisons were built using this template.

Penal reform was becoming increasingly popular. Religious groups like the Quakers and the Evangelicals were highly influential in promoting ideas of reform through personal redemption. In 1866, admirers of John Howard founded the Howard Association – which would later be renamed the Howard League for Penal Reform.

In 1877, prisons were brought under the control of the Prison Commission. For the first time even local prisons were controlled centrally. At this time prison was seen primarily as a means to deter offending. This was a movement away from the reforming ideals of the past.

'Religious groups like the Quakers and the Evangelicals were highly influential in promoting ideas of reform through personal redemption.'

The Prison Act 1898 reasserted reformation as the main role of prison regimes and in many ways this legislation set the tone for prison policy today. It led to a dilution of the separate system, the abolition of hard labour, and established the idea that prison work should be productive, not least for the prisoners, who should be able to earn their livelihood on release.

In the twentieth century the development of the criminal justice system continued.

The Church of England Temperance Society and other voluntary societies appointed missionaries to the London Police Courts during the late nineteenth century. From this developed the system of releasing offenders on the condition that they kept in touch with the missionary and accepted guidance. In 1907, this supervision was given a statutory basis which allowed courts to appoint and employ probation officers. The Probation Order, introduced by the Probation Service in 1907, was the first community sentence. Over the course of the century the use of such community sentences, as an alternative to custody, would increase. Supervision by a probation officer, unpaid work in the community, and eventually drug treatment and the use of restorative justice, would form the elements of these community sentences.

The borstal system was introduced in the Prevention of Crime Act 1908, recognising that young people should have separate prison establishments from adults. Borstal training involved a regime based on hard physical work, technical and educational instruction and a strong moral atmosphere.

In 1933, the first open prison was built at New Hall Camp near Wakefield. The theory behind the open prison was summed up in the words of one penal reform, Sir Alex Paterson: 'You cannot train a man for freedom under conditions of captivity'.

The Probation Order, introduced by the Probation Service in 1907, was the first community sentence.

The Criminal Justice Act 1948 abolished penal servitude, hard labour and flogging. It also presented a comprehensive system for the punishment and treatment of offenders. Prison was still at the centre of the system, but the institutions took many different forms including remand centres, detention centres and borstal institutions.

1965 saw the Murder (Abolition of Death Penalty) Act passed in Parliament.

In the 1990s, there was a political turn in favour of a more punitive approach to crime and justice. The 'prison works' movement was embraced by both Conservative and Labour governments and resulted in a steady rise in the numbers of people behind bars.

At the same time, market reforms were introduced into the justice system. Prisons were introduced which were designed, financed, built and run by private companies.

So far, in the twenty-first century, this trend of rising prison numbers and marketisation has continued. In 2014, the old Probation Service was split into two and much of it was privatised under the Transforming Rehabilitation programme. In the meantime, the politics of 'prison works' and the politics of austerity are in conflict with each other. There is an opportunity once more for meaningful reform.

Criminal Justice Statistics quarterly, England and Wales, year ending December 2018 (annual)

Main points

1.59 million individuals dealt with by the criminal justice system (CJS).

The total number of individuals formally dealt with by the CJS in England and Wales has been declining since 2015 and fell 3% in the latest year to a record low (since 1970).

1.38 million defendants were prosecuted in 2018.

Down 2% since 2017. Decreases were seen in all offence groups except possession of weapons (up 4%) and summary motoring offences (up 3%).

The conviction ratio remained broadly stable at 87% overall.

Increases were seen in some offence groups including sexual offences, possession of weapons and fraud offences, decreases were observed in other offence groups including robbery and theft offences.

The proportion of defendants remanded on bail has continued to fall.

In the latest year, the number of defendants remanded on bail by the Police decreased by 24%, while the number remanded in custody decreased 7%. A similar trend was observed at courts.

The custody rate was 7% and the average custodial sentence length was 17.3 months.

Over the last decade the custody rate has remained stable, however the number sentenced to immediate custody has decreased since 2011, those that did received a longer average custodial sentence length increasing from 13.3 months in 2008 to 17.3 months in 2018.

Offenders with long criminal careers now account for nearly two-fifths of the offending population.

Since 2010, the proportion of offenders with a long criminal career (more than 15 previous cautions or convictions) has increased. In 2018, nearly two-fifths (37%) of the offending population had a long criminal career; an increase of 10 percentage points since 2008.

Out of court disposals

The use of out of court disposals* continues to decline, with a 64% fall since 2008. In 2018, a total of 219,000 received a caution, cannabis/khat warning, community resolution or penalty notice for disorder.

* Out of court disposals are a way of dealing with low-level offences that do not merit prosecution at court. Penalty notices and police cautions are examples out of court disposals.

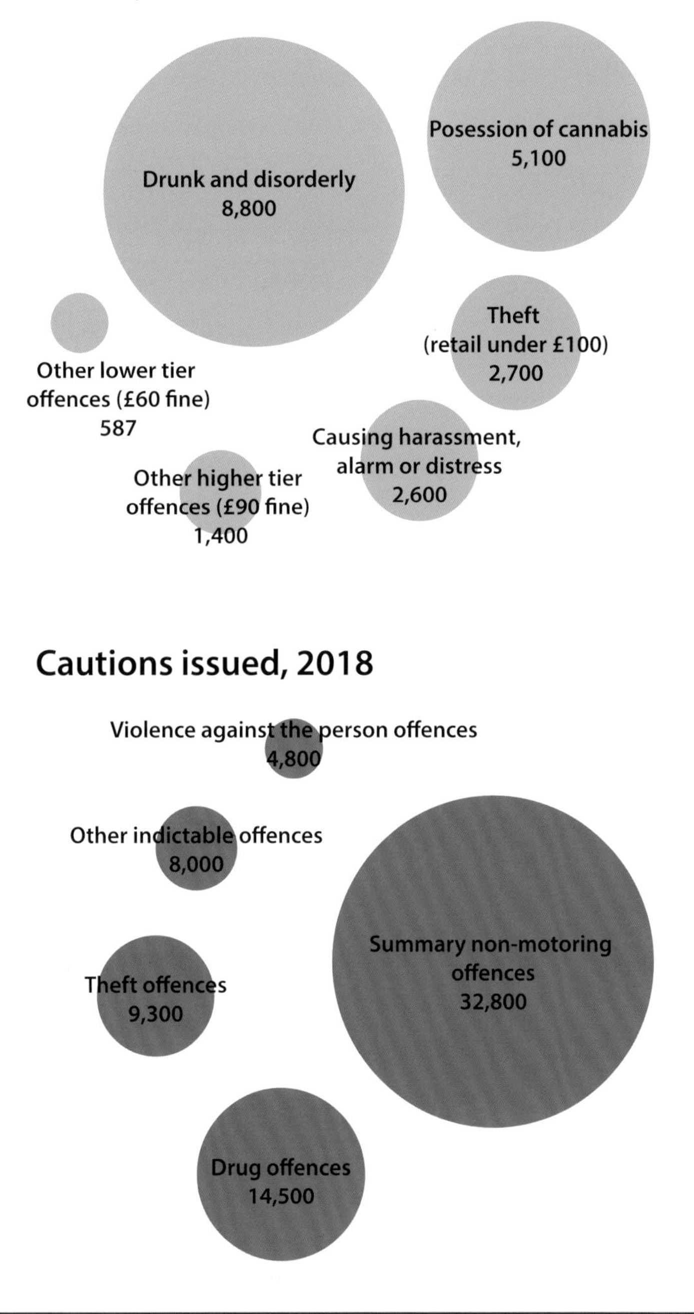

Prosecutions and convictions

1.38 million defendants were prosecuted at magistrates' courts in 2018, 62% over the latest year and 616% since 2008. Decreases were seen across all offences groups apart from possession of weapons, 54% and summary motoring offences, 53%.

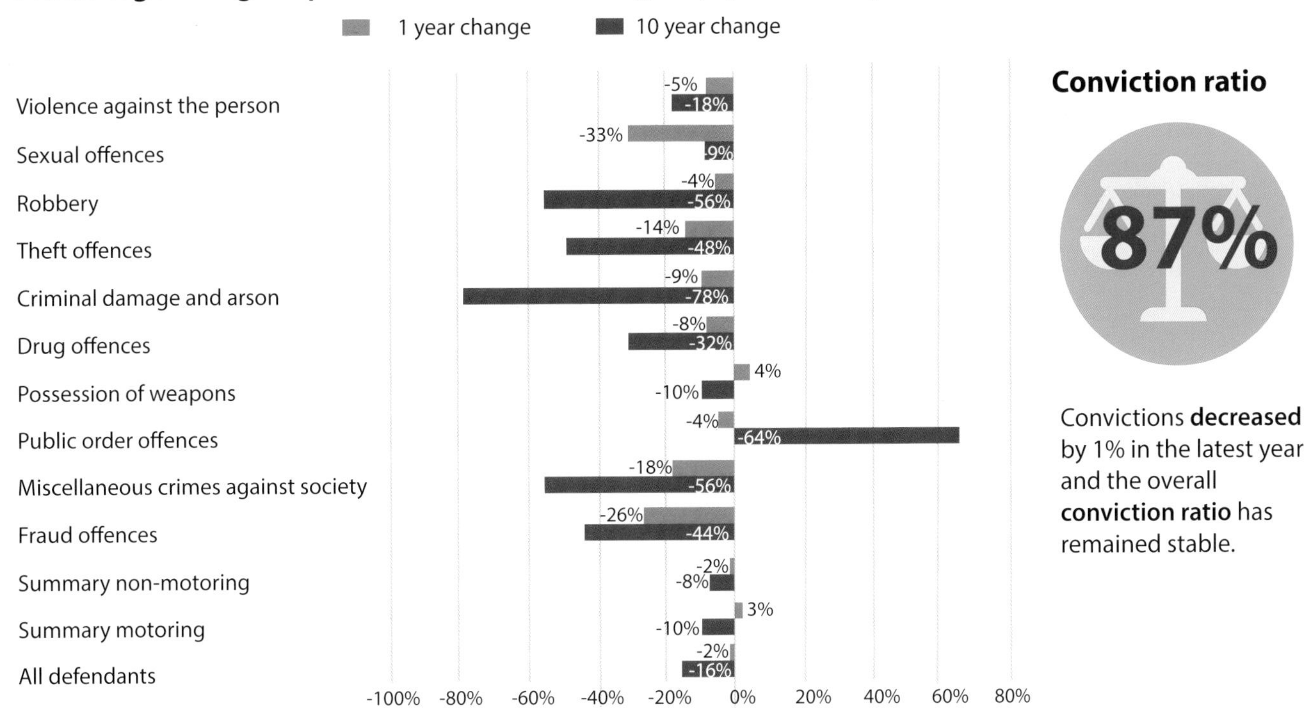

Convictions **decreased** by 1% in the latest year and the overall **conviction ratio** has remained stable.

Remands

The proportion of defendants remanded on bail has continued to fall. The number of defendants remanded on bail by the Police decreased by 24%20, while the number remanded in custody decreased 7%. A similar trend was observed at courts.

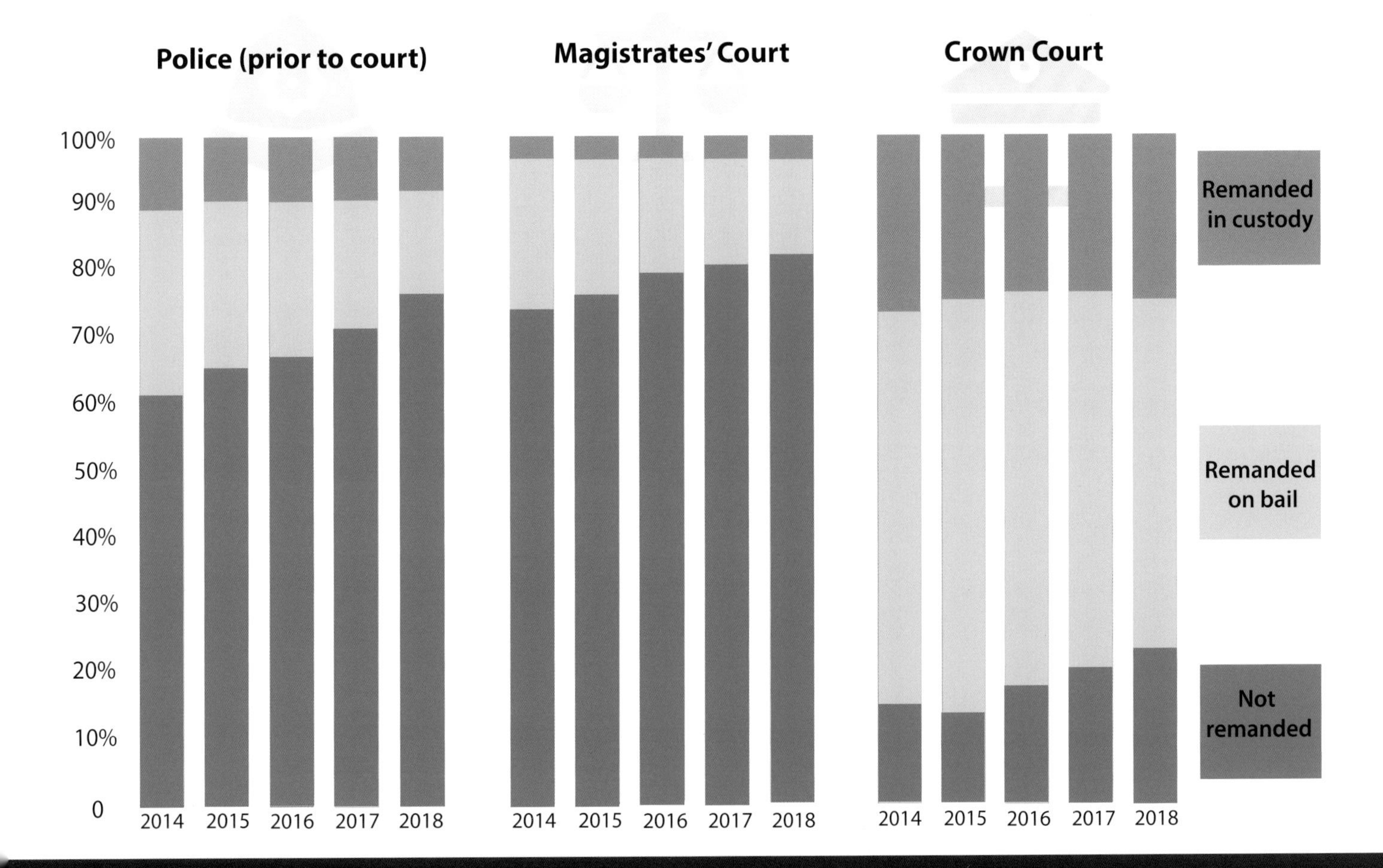

Sentencing

Compared to 2017, the number of **offenders sentenced** at all courts **fell by 1%** to **1.19 million. Fines** remain the most common sentence.

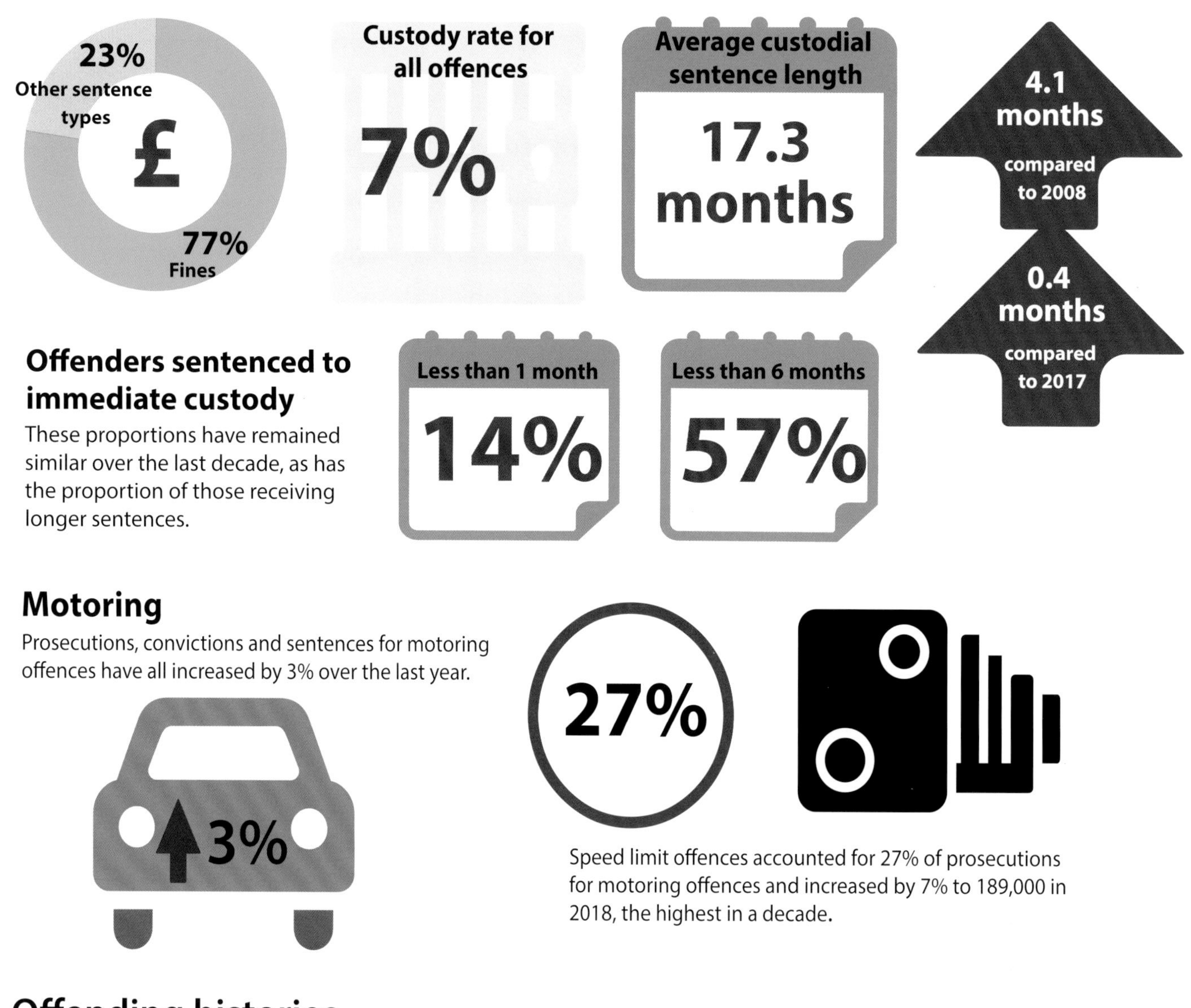

Offenders sentenced to immediate custody

These proportions have remained similar over the last decade, as has the proportion of those receiving longer sentences.

Motoring

Prosecutions, convictions and sentences for motoring offences have all increased by 3% over the last year.

Speed limit offences accounted for 27% of prosecutions for motoring offences and increased by 7% to 189,000 in 2018, the highest in a decade.

Offending histories

Offenders with long criminal careers now account for nearly two-fifths (37%) of the offending population, an increase of 10 percentage points since 2008.

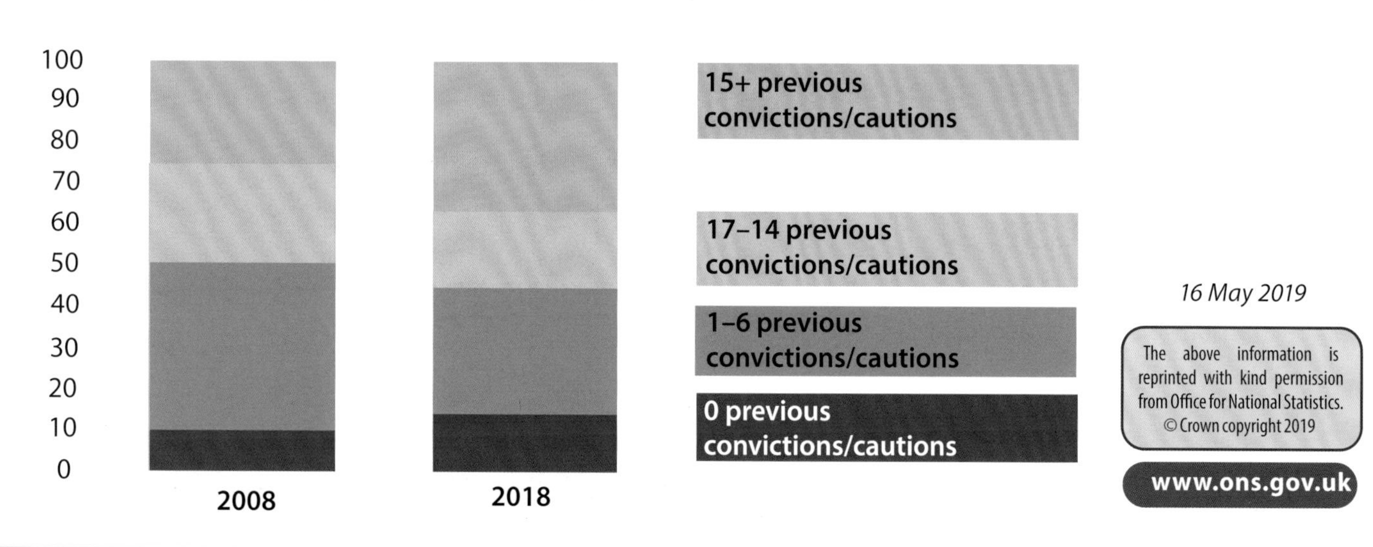

16 May 2019

www.ons.gov.uk

England and Wales have the highest prison rates in Western Europe amid 'botched reforms'

The rate of people being sent to prison in England and Wales has been branded as 'shameful' by Prison Reform Trust.

More people are being sent to prison in England and Wales every year than anywhere else in western Europe.

The rate of people being sent to prison in England and Wales, which has been branded as 'shameful' is around twice as high as in Germany and roughly three times that of Italy and Spain, the Prison Reform Trust found.

This amounted to more than 140,000 admissions into prison in England and Wales in 2017, the most recent year data are available for. The trust's analysis suggests there are nearly 240 prison admissions for every 100,000 people in England and Wales each year.

Prison admission rates

Per 100,000 population

England & Wales*	238
Northern Ireland	222
Denmark	196
Norway	162
France	143
Germany	121
Italy	80
Spain	71

*prison admission rates for Scotland were not available at the time of printing

Source: Prison Reform Trust

The trust's analysis, which used the latest available Council of Europe annual penal statistics, also showed:

- At more than at 82,400, the prison population in England and Wales is nearly 70 per cent higher than three decades ago.
- Each year England and Wales had over 40,000 more admissions to prison than Germany, which has a significantly larger national population.
- More than two-thirds (81 out of 120) of prisons in England and Wales were overcrowded.

'Shameful' record

It blamed an 'addiction to imprisonment', marked by the overuse of short prison sentences and growing use of long terms, as well as botched probation reforms.

The trust's director, Peter Dawson, said: 'These figures show the scale of the challenge that we face in breaking our addiction to imprisonment.

'Planned measures to limit the use of short sentences and correcting failed reforms to probation are both steps in the right direction.

"But our shamefully high prison population rates won't be solved by these alone – a public debate about how we punish the most serious crime is overdue.'

Public debate call

The trust's report says almost half (46 per cent) of people sentenced to prison in England and Wales in 2018 were sentenced to serve six months or less.

Meanwhile, more than two-and-a-half times as many people were sentenced to 10 years or more in 2018 than in 2006, despite levels of serious crime being 'substantially' lower.

England and Wales also have the highest number of indeterminate prisoners (9,441) in western Europe, the report says.

24 June 2019

Stop and search in England and Wales

The use of stops and searches has fallen both in London and across England and Wales, following policy changes a few years ago.

Stops and searches are more likely than ever to result in arrest.

Around 17% of searches resulted in arrests, with 13% resulting in another kind of action in England and Wales in 2017/18.

Black people remain much more likely to be stopped and searched than white people, and this gap has widened in the most recent year we have figures for.

The laws in Scotland and Northern Ireland are different, and they publish their own statistics.

The rules on stop and search have changed

Almost all stops and searches take place under section 1 of the Police and Criminal Evidence Act 1984 and laws associated with that. It's used by police to search people for things like drugs, weapons and stolen property, provided the officer has a reasonable cause to suspect they will find something. The use of section 1 searches had been declining rapidly in the last few years, but fell less sharply this year.

Stops and searches can take place under different laws as well. Those had also been falling rapidly due to changes in policy since 2012 to increase 'fair use' of the powers by the Home Office and Metropolitan Police.

In 2017/18 however, the number of stop and searches carried out under section 60 of the Criminal Justice and Public Order Act increased from 630 to 2,500. Under section 60, a senior police officer can authorise searches for weapons without need for reasonable suspicion in a defined area, to prevent serious violence or to find weapons after an incident. 73% of section 60 searches in England and Wales were carried out by the Metropolitan Police.

For the first time since 2011, stop and searches were also carried out under section 47a (previously s.44) of the Terrorism Act 2000. The majority of these searches (145 of 149) were carried out by the British Transport Police.

In 2014 the Government introduced the 'Best use of stop and search' scheme which aims to increase transparency in the use of stop and search and encourage forces to use the powers more effectively. All forces in England and Wales have now signed up and provide more statistics on the outcome of searches.

The use of stop and search has fallen

The use of stop and search in England and Wales peaked in 2008/09 when over 1.5 million were carried out. It has declined in every year since then. Since 2011/12 – just before the police changes were brought in – stops and searches have fallen by over three-quarters.

Stop and search

Number of stops and searches carried out under three main laws*

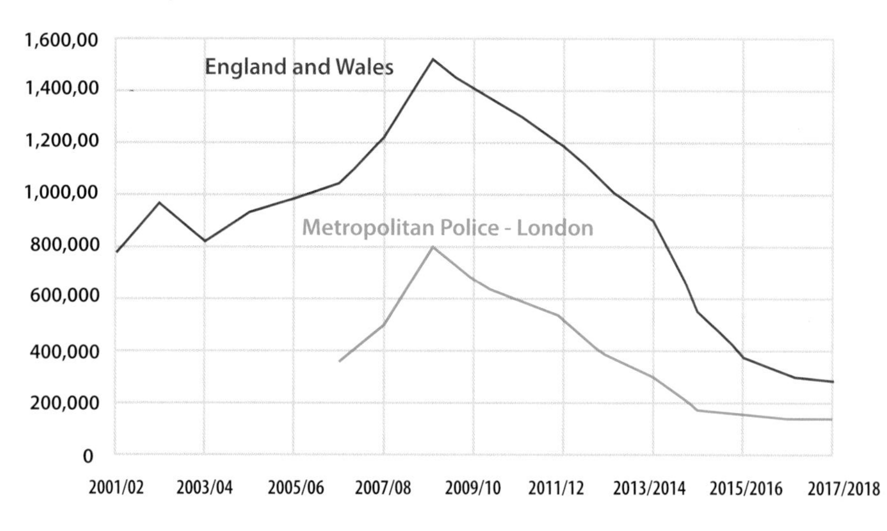

*Overwhelmingly Section 1 of Police and Criminal Evidence Act 1984, also Section 60 of Criminal Justice and Public Order Act 1994 and Section 44/47A of Terrorism Act 2000. Data from before 2009/10 excludes British Transport Police.

Source: Home Office, Stop and Search statistics – police powers and procedures, year ending 31 March 2018

The latest figures put them at just over 280,000 in 2017/18.

London has seen the same pattern. Stops and searches peaked in 2008/09 at nearly 800,000 and fell to just over 130,000 in 2017/18.

The number of stop and searches per person is much higher in London than in the rest of England and Wales, even once you factor in the roughly 2 million people who commute to London during the week.

Stop and search arrest rate

Proportion of all stops and searches resulting in arrests in England and Wales under three main laws*

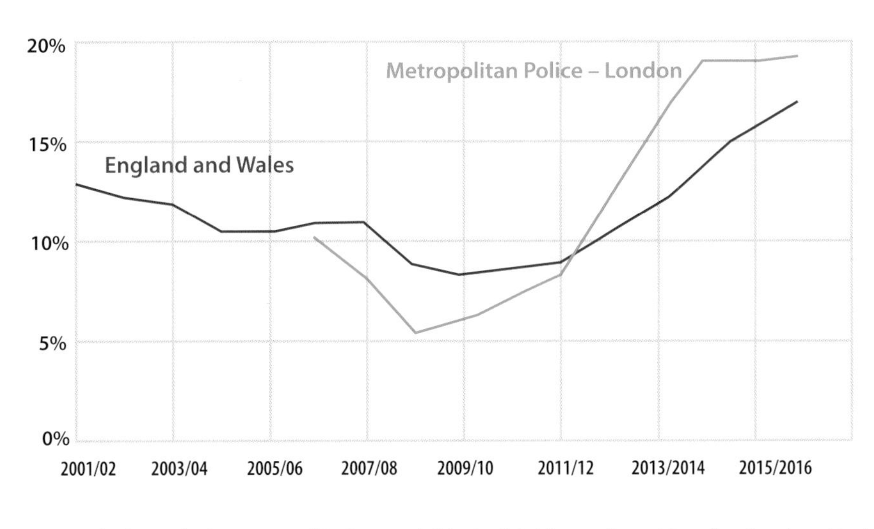

*Overwhelmingly Section 1 of Police and Criminal Evidence Act 1984, also Section 60 of Criminal Justice and Public Order Act 1994 and Section 44/47A of Terrorism Act 2000. Data from before 2009/10 excludes British Transport Police.

Source: Home Office, Stop and Search statistics – police powers and procedures, year ending 31 March 2018

Stops and searches are more likely than ever to result in an arrest

Only 9% of stops and searches resulted in an arrest at the peak of its use in 2008/9. That proportion has increased in the years since and was 17% in 2017/18.

Arrests are more likely in London – with 19% of Metropolitan Police searches resulting in arrest in the same year. The most recent figures suggest the arrest rate may be falling.

While it's tempting to take the higher arrest rate as an indicator of success, Her Majesty's Inspectorate of Constabulary and Fire & Rescue Services note that an arrest isn't necessarily a success, nor is a failure to uncover any wrongdoing necessarily a failure.

Offenders could, for instance, be arrested even if no stolen or prohibited goods are found, because they might react violently to officers or be wanted for another offence.

On the flipside, failing to uncover wrongdoing could be regarded as a success if, without the stop and search powers in place, the person under suspicion would otherwise have been arrested unnecessarily.

A third of stops and searches uncover something relevant

These are called 'positive outcome' searches – which refers to any case where action is taken against people who've been stopped and searched. This includes arrest cases but also covers other resolutions like warnings and Penalty Notices. All cases where there isn't a positive outcome are called 'No Further Actions'.

Across England and Wales, 30% of stops and searches had a positive outcome in 2017/18.

This figure could be higher in reality because some No Further Action cases do involve detentions under the Mental Health Act or informal advice being given when an officer has found something untoward.

The figures are similar for the Metropolitan Police in London. In 2017/18, 60% of stop and searches resulting in a 'positive outcome' were related to drugs offences, 11% to theft, fraud and counterfeit offences, and 9% were for 'weapons, points and blades'.

Outside the Metropolitan Police, police officers find what they're searching for in one out of five cases

Police forces have to report whether the outcome was linked to the reason for the search.

For example, when someone is stopped for a drug search and given a cannabis warning the outcome is linked. If no drugs are found but they're arrested for carrying a weapon the outcome isn't linked. If nothing is found and no action is taken that also isn't counted as linked.

So in England and Wales, officers found what they were searching for in around one in five searches. The reason for

Stop and search: the racial imbalance

How many times as likely black/black British people are to be stopped and searched as white* people across England and Wales.

10 times
9 times
8 times
7 times
6 times
5 times
4 times
3 times
Twice as likely
Just as likely
2010/11 2011/12 2012/2013 2013/2014 2014/2015 2015/2016 2016/2017 2017/2018

*Based on self-defined ethnicity, population based in 2011 census.

Source: Home Office, police powers and procedures, year ending 31 March 2018 the search makes a big difference, with searches for drugs being more successful than stops for weapon searches or going equipped.

They also find that whether someone is white or not makes little difference – the rate is still about 20%.

Again, these cover 'positive outcomes' of stops and searches, but they're different to the figures mentioned in the previous section because they only include cases where the officer found what they were searching for in the first place.

Black people are still more likely to be stopped and searched

The majority of the population is white and the majority of stops and searches involve white people. Per person, black people are more likely to be stopped and searched.

Black people are about nearly 10 times as likely to be stopped and searched as white people. Three in every 1,000 white people were stopped and searched in 2017/18, compared to 29 in every 1,000 black people.

The difference in rates between white and black people has grown since last year. Stops and searches have fallen in the last year overall but those involving white people have fallen faster than those involving black people.

Black people are more likely to be arrested following a stop and search. 21% of stops and searches on black people resulted in an arrest in 2017/18, compared to 16% of those conducted on white people.

We have more figures just for the Metropolitan Police in London covering June 2018 to May 2019.

Black people were four times as likely to be stopped and searched in London as white people – they were stopped 63.4 times per 1,000 people compared to 14.7 times for white people.

People of all ethnicities are more likely to be stopped and searched in London than elsewhere.

Positive outcome rates are similar whatever people's ethnicity is. Around 25% of searches result in some action being taken.

Does stop and search work?

There is little research on whether stop and search prevents and deters crime.

Recent research using ten years of data from the Metropolitan Police found that:

'higher rates of stop and search (under any power) were associated with very slightly lower than expected rates of crime in the following week or month…'

'The inconsistent nature and weakness of these associations, however, provide only limited evidence of stop and search having acted as a deterrent at a borough level. It is possible that stop and search may be more strongly associated with crime at a more local level, assuming it is targeted appropriately in crime hot spots.'

It also found that increasing the use of section 60 powers (stops without reasonable suspicion) did not appear to affect violent crime.

Previous research on the use of section 60 powers to reduce knife crime also found no effect. Some US research has found small effects on some types of crime, and there is evidence that concentrating policing on crime 'hotspots' does deter criminals.

24 June 2019

It'll take more than bobbies on the beat to restore order to lawless Britain

By Rory Geoghegan, Head of Criminal Justice, The Centre for Social Justice.

Leaving the EU is the number one issue for voters, but crime has proven itself capable of being the number two issue this year – and the next Prime Minister must have a bold plan to tackle it. The rise of crime as a political issue speaks to the undeniable rises in knife crime, serious youth violence, and related violence and thuggery – but it also speaks to the virtual demise of proactive crimefighting across large swathes of the country.

The failure to provide adequate resources for this fight exacts a huge price on the poorest communities. Just imagine trying to bring up your kids on a housing estate where criminality and illegal drug use is obvious, explicit and expected.

The addition of 20,000 police officers – as offered by the likely next Prime Minister Boris Johnson – is a welcome step provided he can successfully set them free to fight crime.

However, turning around the rest of our failing criminal justice system, while eminently achievable, will be much harder.

There is a botched and failed part-privatisation and simultaneous part-nationalisation of probation that must be sorted out. Mapping probation back onto police force areas would be a good start, and provide the foundation for local areas, with the support of their elected Mayor or Police and Crime Commissioner, to get on and make a better fist of things.

Meanwhile, our prisons are awash with drugs, record-levels of violence and selfharm. The unwillingness from some to tackle these key issues undermines the real benefits of prison: a secure space in which to address the root causes of criminal behaviour and protect the public.

A recent report by the Centre for Social Justice, *Control, Order, Hope*, sets out how proven body scanner technology, along with real empowerment and accountability for prison governors, would make all the difference. With one in three new prison officers resigning within 12 months, turning our prisons around is vital.

At the same time the 'court reform' programme has seen court closures make justice literally more distant from the communities that are most impacted. A longstanding emphasis on dropping cases and resolving cases swiftly goes against the potential for some courts to focus on community problem solving.

This is far from an exhaustive list – there are many further challenges, from the need to reconceive our approach to anti-social behaviour as crime, to supporting businesses and trade bodies to take greater responsibility for prevention and detection. We must also face down the reality that too much of our criminal justice system has been about ticking boxes rather than securing reductions in crime.

One example of this is the approach to electronic monitoring, where GPS tags will record the movement of offenders to make sure they attend appointments, but their movements will not be screened against recorded crime. While fig leaf arguments over privacy and human rights are used, the real fear is that more crime might be detected and the Ministry of Justice might need more, rather than fewer, prison spaces.

This is the ultimate fudge that has been at the heart of our criminal justice system and politics for decades: an obsession with policy tinkering to manage the prison population number so that it meets an arbitrary value. The tinkering must end. A new Prime Minister must place the emphasis on the nature and quality of what goes on, both in our communities and in our prisons, to cut crime and protect the public – and to ensure that the resources are there to drive crime down, even if it means more prison spaces.

Now is not just the time for us to take back control of our laws and borders, it's also time to reassert the rule of law and to offer up a serious plan to tackle crime.

5 July 2019

www.telegraph.co.uk

Key Facts

- The Crime Survey for England and Wales (CSEW) indicated a continuing rise in fraud with the latest estimates showing a 15% increase, driven by a 17% rise in 'bank and credit account fraud'. (page 1)
- Police statistics have shown that knife and gun-related crimes increased by an overwhelming 14 per cent just last year. (page 4)
- The Youth Justice Statistics, published in January 2018, show that there was a staggering 14,500 new entrants into the Youth Justice System. (page 4)
- The number of police officers in England and Wales has fallen by over 20,000 between March 2010 and March 2018. (page 5)
- The Office for National Statistics said that in the year to December 2018, 732 lives were lost to homicide, compared with 690 the previous year. The figure is the highest number recorded since 2008. Homicide includes murder, manslaughter, corporate manslaughter and infanticide. (page 6)
- According to the Crime Survey for England and Wales, violent crime peaked in 1995 and has fallen by over two-thirds since then. In recent years, those falls have largely flattened out. (page 8)
- The most commonly committed micro-crime is paying someone cash-in-hand knowing that they won't pay tax, with (43 per cent of YouGov pollsters confessed to this micro-crime). (page 15)
- In the year ending March 2019, there were around 47,000 (selected) offences involving a knife or sharp instrument in England and Wales. (page 17)
- If you are aged between 12 and 17 years and are caught twice with a knife, you are likely to face at least a four months detention and training order. (page 18)
- It is illegal to sell a knife to anybody under the age of 18. (page 18)
- Possession of a knife carries a prison sentence of up to four years even if it's not used. (page 19)
- The overall crime rate rose by eight per cent to 5.95 million offences for the year ending March 2019, according to the Office for National Statistics (ONS). (page 22)
- Knife crime rose by up to 50 per cent in rural areas in the past year (2019) as violence spread from cities, fuelled by county lines drug gangs, official figures show. (page 22)
- London, has 16 of the top 25 areas for knife crime (more than one crime per 10,000 people). (page 24)
- In England, there were 5,053 knife assaults recorded in 2017–18, an increase of 14% since 2016–17 and 39% higher than in 2014–15. Just over one in five knife offenders are between the ages of 10 and 17. (page 25)
- John Howard was the first penal reformer. In 1777, Howard (namesake of the Howard League) condemned the prison system as disorganised, barbaric and filthy. He called for wide-ranging reforms including the installation of paid staff, outside inspection, a proper diet and other necessities for prisoners. (page 30)
- In 1799, the Pentitentiary Act specified that gaols should be built for one inmate per cell and operate on a silent system with continuous labour. (page 31)
- The first national penitentiary was completed at Millbank in London, in 1816. (page 31)
- The Probation Order, introduced by the Probation Service in 1907, was the first community sentence. (page 31)
- The borstal system was introduced in the Prevention of Crime Act 1908, recognising that young people should have separate prison establishments from adults. (page 31)
- 1965 saw the Murder (Abolition of Death Penalty) Act passed in Parliament. (page 31)
- 1.59 million individuals were dealt with by the criminal justice system (CJS) in 2018. (page 32)
- The latest available Council of Europe annual penal statistics, showed that at more than 82,400, the prison population in England and Wales is nearly 70 per cent higher than three decades ago. (page 35)
- In 2017/18, however the number of stop and searches carried out under section 60 of the Criminal Justice and Public Order Act increased from 630 to 2,500. Under section 60, a senior police officer can authorise searches for weapons without need for reasonable suspicion in a defined area, to prevent serious violence or to find weapons after an incident. 73% of section 60 searches in England and Wales were carried out by the Metropolitan Police. (page 36)
- Black people are about nearly 10 times as likely to be stopped and searched as white people. Three in every 1,000 white people were stopped and searched in 2017/18, compared to 29 in every 1,000 black people. (page 38)

County lines
'County Lines' is a term used to describe criminal gangs from big cities who expand their operations to smaller towns. They groom and exploit children and vulnerable people to traffick and sell drugs for them.

Crime
Crime may be defined as an act or omission prohibited or punished by law. A 'criminal offence' includes any infringement of the criminal law, from homicide to riding a bicycle without lights. What is classified as a crime is supposed to reflect the values of society and to reinforce those values. If an act is regarded as harmful to society or its citizens, it is often, but not always, classified as a criminal offence.

Crime Survey for England & Wales (CSEW)
The Crime Survey for England and Wales (CSEW) is an organised study of national crime trends. It measures the levels and types of crime in England and Wales by asking people about whether they or members of their households have experienced any crimes in the past year.

Criminal Justice System (CJS)
The criminal justice system is the set of agencies and processes established by governments to control crime and impose penalties on those who violate law.

Cuckooing
The process through which county lines operators take over a local property to use as a base for their criminal activity. The operators usually target and exploit vulnerable people such as those dependent on drugs, with mental health issues, or the elderly. Through the use of violence, intimidation, or coercion (i.e. by offering money or drugs in exchange for use of their property), the operators then take over the property, sometimes rendering the victim homeless in the process.

Custody
In criminal terminology, being 'in custody' refers to someone being held in spite of their wishes, either by the police while awaiting trial (remanded in custody), or, having received a custodial sentence, in prison or other secure accommodation. If someone has spent time on remand, that time is taken off their prison sentence.

Drill and Grime
A genre of music often linked to gang violence due to its lyrical content.

Howard League for Penal Reform
The Howard League for Penal Reform is the oldest penal reform charity in the UK. It was established in 1866 and is named after John Howard, one of the first prison reformers.

Knife crime
'Knife' crime is crime involving a knife or an object with a blade or a sharp instrument. It's a crime to threaten someone with a knife or carry a knife as a weapon in a robbery or burglary. Police can search you if they think you're carrying a knife.

Public order offence
There is a wide range of offences set out in the Public Order Act 1986, which make many different kinds of behaviour criminal offences. They usually refer to the use of or threat of violence or harassment towards someone else, in a public place.

Runners
The term describing the vulnerable children and adults who are recruited by gangs to transport drugs and cash across rural and suburban counties.

Stop and search
There are different types of stop and search.

Under section 1 of the Police and Criminal Evidence Act, stop and search requires officers to show they have 'reasonable grounds' to believe you're carrying a prohibited item before subjecting you to an invasive public search.

But under section 60 of the Criminal Justice and Public Order Act, officers can, for a certain time period, carry out searches without ANY 'reasonable grounds'.

Street gangs
Criminal groups concerned with perpetuating a threat of violence or harm across a geographical area related to their main activities. Gangs tend to be less organised or co-ordinated than organised crime groups, but their criminal activity often overlaps.

Activities

Brainstorming

- In small groups, discuss what you know about crime and justice in the UK. Consider the following points:
  - What is the age of criminal responsibility in the UK?
  - Have crime rates gone up or down in recent years?
  - Which crimes do you see covered the most in the news?
  - Which crimes particularly affect young people today? Give some examples. Which crimes worry you the most?

Research

- Research crime rates in the United States and make some notes on how they compare to the UK. How do US gun crime statistics compare to those of the UK?
- Look through a selection of newspapers or news websites from your local area and make a list of all the crimes reported in them. Which crimes seem to be the most common?
- Find out about a crime-prevention scheme in your local area that has been designed to either:
  - help rehabilitate offenders
  - support victims of crime, or
  - reduce crime rates.

  Write some notes and feedback to the rest of your class.
- Read the article on page 8. What are the main three sources of data used to measure crime rates?
- How many organised crime gangs are there currently operating in the UK? (see page 11)
- Take a look at the article on page 23. Which county in the UK saw the largest increase in knife crime in 2019?

Design

- Design a poster or a series of online banners aimed at young people warning them about the dangers of carrying a knife.
- Choose one of the articles in this book and create an illustration to highlight the key themes/message of your chosen article.
- Design a leaflet that gives young people information and advice about the dangers of getting involved in gangs and drug dealing.
- Design an app that could be used to prevent crime.

Oral

- Look at the statistics presented in the Crime Survey for England and Wales (pages 1–3). Why has there been a significant rise in Public Order Offences over recent years? In small groups, discuss the reasons you think have contributed to this trend.
- As a class, re-enact a scenario where a street gang tries to recruit a young person into their operation. Think about and discuss some of the reasons why a young person might be tempted to join a gang. What are the attractions? Is it always a choice?
- Choose one of the illustrations from this book and, with a partner, discuss what you think the artist was trying to portray.
- In pairs, recreate a 'restorative justice' scenario, in which the victim of a robbery meets the person who robbed them.
- In small groups, look at the list of micro crimes in the article on pages 15–16. Do they surprise you? Have you ever knowingly or unknowingly committed one these micro crimes? Are there any other micro crimes you are aware of?

Reading/writing

- Write an advice guide for young victims of crime, explaining how they can report a crime and what support they will receive afterwards.
- Do you think TV series such as *Top Boy* glamourise crime and criminal activity? What about rap, grime and drill music? Give reasons for your answer.
- Write a short story about someone recently released following a strech in prison and their attempt to rebuild their life. What are the biggest challenges they they face?
- Do you think the police in England should be able to carry guns? Write a blog post exploring your opinion.
- The use of section 60 (stopping and searching a person without reasonable suspicion) is very controversial. Write a short article about the pros and cons of 'Stop and Search' as a crime deterrent.

Index

Acknowledgements

The publisher is grateful for permission to reproduce the material in this book. While every care has been taken to trace and acknowledge copyright, the publisher tenders its apology for any accidental infringement or where copyright has proved untraceable. The publisher would be pleased to come to a suitable arrangement in any such case with the rightful owner.

Images

Cover image courtesy of iStock. All other images courtesy of Pixabay and Unsplash, except

Icons

Icons on pages 33, 34 and 35 were made by Freepik, Nikita Golubev and Smashicons from www.flaticon.com.

Illustrations

Don Hatcher: pages 19 & 38. Simon Kneebone: pages 4 & 29. Angelo Madrid: pages 12 & 30.

Additional acknowledgements

With thanks to the Independence team: Shelley Baldry, Danielle Lobban, Jackie Staines and Jan Sunderland.

Tracy Biram

Cambridge, January 2020